Intuition

Intuition

Awakening Your Inner Guide

Judee Gee

BARNES & NOBLE

NEW YORK

To my son Graham,
who, in his early years was obliged to accompany me along my path
and whose presence in my life has taught me more about love,
wisdom, and the path of authenticity than he can ever imagine.

And to all my clients and students,
whose presence has allowed me to develop my own intuition,
I thank you for your trust and willingness to follow the way.

Contents

1

INTUITION: THE BIRTHRIGHT OF EVERY BEING

2

THE DIMENSION OF BODY, MIND, AND BEING:
UNDERSTANDING AND TRANSFORMING OUR INNER WORLD

3

DEVELOPING YOUR INTUITION:
CREATING THE INNER STRUCTURE

4

UTILIZING YOUR INTUITION

5

UTILIZING YOUR INTUITION WITH OTHERS

6

INTUITION AND EVOLUTION OF THE SOUL

EXERCISES AND MEDITATIONS

LIST OF ILLUSTRATIONS

Acknowledgments

Gratitude is a sweet nectar, true nourishment for the heart. At the completion of this project, I understand more deeply how writing is a truly solitary affair. The gratitude I feel in my heart goes toward the people who formed an essential part of my life during the writing of this manuscript, and who, each in their own way, supported me in this task.

I am grateful to Jean-Louis Abrassart, who encouraged me from the beginning and helped me through difficult moments. I acknowledge him for his commitment to the path, and for the strength of his convictions, which helped me to clarify my own.

To Véronique Groux de Mieri, my friend and translator for the original French edition, for her much appreciated collaboration and wicked sense of humor.

I acknowledge with gratitude and appreciation for their contribution, all the teachers of the intuition team in France since the beginning: Vanessa Mielczarek, Michèle Isorez, Gérard Belaud, Odile Besançon, Gilles Bouilliez, Magali Amir, Arnaud Sebal, Claire Guichard, Jill Mackechnie, Guy Ravanel, and Jean-Loup Champetier de Ribes.

For their collaboration with the illustrations and photos I thank Geneviève Dindart, François Chomicki, and Studio Eclipse, Annecy. With special thanks to Marie-Françoise, "super-secretary," and to Vanessa Jones and Sally Rush for their scrupulous corrections of the manuscript. I am very grateful to Deva Visarjan and Alain Roux, two special people I have been privileged to teach with over the years, who have taught me what inspirational collaboration can be.

And to the beloved souls I have been journeying with more recently, into inner worlds—David, Gilly, Eva, Robin, Annetta, Michael, Claire, and Nemi—I thank you for your presence, your *écoute,* and your spirit. Eirik I thank, for sacred Love.

Introduction

The infinite mystery of the gift of intuition has always fascinated me. The task of giving it tangible form has been one of my primary preoccupations since I first discovered the irrefutable evidence of my own intuition in 1980 at Heartsong School for Psychic Perception in Berkeley, California. The revelation of my intuitive gift, made possible through the teachings I received, deeply and permanently transformed my perception of myself, of others, and of the world in which we exist.

The discovery of my intuition was, in fact, a rediscovery of myself. Reflecting back on myself before I was re-aligned with my intuition, I see someone fragmented into many morsels, into many different facets, always searching, looking, seeking for something lost, for something precious and very essential to my fundamental well-being and sense of Self. I see myself slowly reassembling the fragments, bringing myself together and remembering who I was. By reconciling with my intuition, I suddenly brought everything together into a whole. The rediscovery of my capacity to access and perceive the truth within myself created a deep healing in my heart and a profound sense of coming home to myself.

I always assumed that intuition was a gift for a privileged few. The realization that it is an inner capacity waiting to be awakened in all beings was a tremendous inspiration to me. I knew immediately that I had found my way, my path. I knew with certainty that it was part of my purpose to teach intuition development in the world. I also understood that I had "lost" and then rediscovered my own intuition so that I could better understand and assist others in their own process of inner awakening.

I love intuition. I love its mystery, its depth, and its truth. Guiding others to the revelation of their own intuition is a delicate, powerful, and blessed work, a process in which I participate with respect and gratitude.

Throughout my years as a healer and psychotherapist, I have understood that the four burning questions which motivate people on a path of personal transformation and spiritual development are: Who am I? Why am I here? What is happening? Where am I going?

These questions create the spiritual quest, the search. The moment we begin to ask ourselves these questions, we trigger the initiatory journey within ourselves and our lives become the means through which we explore and discover the answers we seek.

It is impossible to find the answer to these questions with the rational mind. We may begin to answer through a logical process of rational deduction, but we will quickly discover that the reasonable answers of the mind are flat, limited, and without depth or inspiration. We are obliged to reach deeper, to come back to ourselves in a different manner, in order to explore the possible answers to these questions.

The gift of intuition is the gift of remembering, of knowing and of belonging. Intuition brings us to these questions and, loving soul that she is, she also brings us to the answers—showing us that the answers are always there, preciously protected, until such time as we are ready to discover them.

Intuition is our birthright, a blessed birthright, evidence of divinity incarnate in physical form. Thanks to our intuition, we can find our place and purpose in this world and realize our deepest potential. Thanks to our intuition, we can reconcile ourselves with a living, loving, guiding presence we perceive with our inner senses. We can heal ourselves and we can participate in the healing process of others and the healing of our world, our home.

I sincerely hope that reading this book will help you to receive the blessing of your intuition into your life.

1

INTUITION: THE BIRTHRIGHT OF EVERY BEING

CHAPTER ONE

What Is Intuition?

Intuition is a mysterious, powerful, and subtle ability that every human being possesses and can develop. It is an ability we are born with—an innate capacity that exists within us. By our own choice, we can ignore it or follow it, neglect it or nourish it.

The function of the intuition is not imperative to our survival but it does hold a place of tremendous importance in relation to our physical and spiritual well-being, our creative self-expression, and our ability to understand ourselves, others, and the experience of life itself.

The *Oxford English Dictionary* defines intuition as "the quick perception of truth without conscious attention or reasoning; knowledge from within; instinctive knowledge or feeling. . . ." Intuition, by its very nature, is not a function of the conscious mind. It is "quick," "without reasoning," "without conscious attention." Intuition is a function that springs from a deeper source than the linear, rational mind. With our intuition, we can perceive the truth; we can perceive the real nature, the true state, of a person, a situation, or ourselves. This perception, this understanding, is something that comes from within us; it is something akin to instinct and feeling.

INTUITION IS CONSCIOUSNESS

Intuition is linked to the function of the subconscious mind—the imaginative hemisphere of the mind—which operates from a global, unified perspective. Intuition is not, however, actually a function of the subconscious mind. Intuitive perception is a function of the consciousness of the being, acting through the mind, through the subconscious and conscious levels of mental awareness. The intuition springs from a deeper source than the mind, even though its transmissions are received and integrated by the subconscious mind and translated through the conscious mind.

INTUITION IS AWARENESS

We can better understand the intuition by relating it to the capacities of instinct and intelligence. If we imagine that instinct is a function of the awareness of the body, and intelligence is a function of the

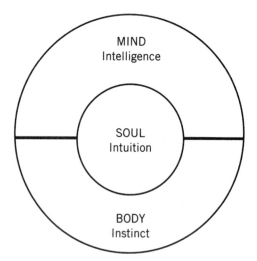

Figure 1. Instinct, intelligence, intuition.

awareness of the mind, then we can understand intuition as a function of the awareness of the soul and spirit.

Intuition is the expression of the awareness of the soul, the consciousness of the soul. In the soul, we find the aspect of the human being that is immortal and wise, the being who has its origins in light and has never lost the capacity to enter into contact with a larger vision, a higher truth.

INTUITION, SOUL, AND SPIRIT

Beyond our identity as a personality, beyond our human dimension of the body/mind, we exist above all as a being composed of a soul and a spirit. It is the presence (soul) and awareness (spirit) of this being which animates our body/mind.

The soul manifests the feminine nature of our being, searching for relation, meaning, feeling, and fusion. Incarnation into a human body and an earthly life provide the soul with a diversity of experiences which generate the gradual accumulation of wisdom. Evolution occurs over time through the interactions of the soul with other living beings. During many successive incarnations, challenges are faced, lessons are learned, and qualities are developed, bringing to the soul the diversity of experiences needed to become a realized being.

Feminine by nature, the soul receives, absorbs, and integrates the experience of her existence through a predominant framework of sensation and feeling. Receptive and passive, discovering her nature through the reflection of the other, the soul drinks life, nourishing her thirst for evolution and realization by embracing the lessons life brings to her. In the certainty of her immortality, the soul can go far in her search for diversity of experience. Wisdom is the goal of the soul; interrelationships are her means. The worlds of feeling and emotion are the domains of the soul. It is through our own inner world of feeling that we can reconnect with the deepness of our soul-self.

The spirit is the manifestation of the masculine aspect of our being. The spirit is pure consciousness, awareness incarnate. By nature detached, the spirit observes, perceives, and witnesses. While present and available to the unfolding process of life, the spirit nonetheless maintains a certain position of distance in relation to the events experienced. The spirit perceives life with a large perspective, with the global vision of a being aware of his origins, of his original nature, and of his relationship to the source of all life. The spirit is aware of his divine nature, and also of his immortality.

Masculine in essence, the spirit is expressive, dynamic, and active. The spirit generates and creates, penetrating the world of matter with the charismatic vitality of his presence. The spirit perceives reality with depth and lucidity, and acts in the world with certainty and true power. The qualities of the spirit find their expression through the consciousness of the mind and the action of thought through physical matter.

It is the presence of soul and spirit incarnate in the human form which gives birth to our intuitive function. Intuition is the means by which our being perceives reality—the means through which our being can act on and interact with that same reality.

Our intuitive self is our most evolved self, our highest self, a being both aware and conscious. The intuitive self perceives the actions of the personality (body/mind) in the world and observes the unfolding of life's experiences with lucidity and attention.

If we wish to understand the dynamics of ourselves, of another, or of an event with intuitive depth and insight, we must enter into contact with this being in order to receive the insights of its perceptions.

INTUITION IS INNER GUIDANCE

Our intuition helps us to know and understand ourselves and our purpose in life. It functions as a guide, helping us develop our highest creative potential. It "points" us in directions which encourage us to develop further and to explore deeper, to discover and know ourselves more fully.

It is healthy and natural to be able to delve deeply into the true nature of the reality that surrounds us. It is natural to be able to understand how people, situations, and events exist in relation to each other. It is our birthright to be able to perceive our appropriate place in the world and to understand the personal, creative contribution we can make in our life.

Before we can benefit fully from our intuition, we must enter into contact with it—we must recognize its manner of functioning and learn to communicate with it. We must develop a relationship with it and nourish this relationship with our attention. With time and attention, we can learn how our intuition transmits insights and truths, and more clearly understand how we can receive and translate them.

CHAPTER TWO

The Four Pathways of Intuitive Function

E ven though the function of the intuition is experienced in a unique fashion for each person, there are essentially four pathways through which its guidance can be transmitted: clairsentience (clear feeling), clairaudience (clear hearing), clairvoyance (clear seeing), and knowingness (direct perception).

CLAIRSENTIENCE

Clairsentience, or clear feeling, is the experience of receiving intuitive information as sensation and/or emotional feelings in your physical body. This information can take the form of an instinctive reaction or response that creates a notable physical change and movement in the body, or it may be received in a more subtle manner, acting on your inner physical world of sensation. Your intuitive self can communicate with you by creating sensations (warmth, cold, tingling, twitching, tightening, relaxing) within your physical body. These physical sensations will indicate something significant to you if you bring your attention and awareness to their existence.

Clear feeling is the most frequent pathway through which the function of the intuition is recognized and understood. It is with your clairsentience that you "feel" the emotional state of someone

else, that you "understand" their pain, their joy, their suffering.
Because of your clairsentience, you may feel depressed after being in
the presence of a depressed friend, or your spirits may improve if you
spend some time with a friend who is full of enthusiasm and projects
for the future.

Your clairsentience gives you the ability to "feel" a situation and
to understand an atmosphere. This ability alerts you when you are in
a potentially dangerous situation, so that you can remove yourself or
change your behavior in an appropriate way to avoid the danger.

It is with your clairsentience that you monitor your emotional
relationships with others and modify your responses to maintain a
state of balance and harmony. With the help of clairsentience, you
feel the mood of another person and modify your behavior to maintain your rapport. If someone close to you is angry, you may feel their
anger as a tightness or a pain in your solar plexus, or as a tension in
the forehead and jaws. Regardless of whether other people express or
deny their anger, your body is relaying relevant information to you
about the truth of their current state of being.

Likewise, if you are stressed and nervous, other people may
become drained, nervous, or perhaps develop a headache by being in
your presence. Even if you do not recognize the symptoms of stress
or nervous fatigue in your own body, other people can experience
them when, clairsentiently, they enter into intuitive contact and rapport with you.

The less you are in contact with yourself—with your inner emotional state and your physical body—the less you can be in contact
with your clairsentience. The more you are emotionally repressed
and physically blocked, the more your capacity for clairsentience is
repressed and blocked. The more you are in touch with your physical body and your own emotional state, the more your clairsentience
can function for you in your life.

Once your capacity for clear feeling on an intuitive level is developed, it becomes an invaluable tool that can assist you in all of life's

situations. However, when you initially bring your awareness to this capacity, you may discover that it causes you confusion and moments of self-doubt as you realize the difficulties you have in discerning the difference between your proper feelings and the feelings of others. If you experience this confusion of differentiation, pay particular attention to the exercises of inner preparation which focus on grounding, centering, and creating a personal boundary.

CLAIRAUDIENCE

Clairaudience, or clear hearing, describes the function of your intuition through auditory channels, in the sense that you hear information. In this pathway of expression, your intuitive self speaks to you and you receive messages as words. You may hear an inner voice with a particular tone or accent, or it may be a voice resembling your own. It may change; it may be several different voices. Clairaudience is also known as telepathy, or communication through the mind. Sometimes, you may have a thought about someone and, that very day, you receive a telephone call or a letter from the person. Or the telephone rings and, before you pick it up, you hear the name of the person who is calling inside your head. On answering the telephone, you discover you are correct. Perhaps you have a problem or a question and are in the process of reflecting on this problem when you open a book and there, in front of your eyes, is the answer to your question—a written response that acts as a useful guidance for you. All information and guidance that you receive in an auditory (verbal) fashion is an expression of the function of your intuitive clairaudience.

The indications of a clairaudient talent are most often perceived in someone who is a gifted communicator. If you are confident in your ability to express yourself and you have trust in the truth you communicate, if you are at ease within yourself as you share what you perceive with others, then your intuition very likely functions through the framework of clairaudience.

If you have a tendency to doubt your communicative ability, if you have difficulty listening to and hearing others and in understanding the expression of others, then this function may be blocked. Chronic throat problems, neck tension, teeth and jaw problems, and upper-back pain are also indications of a repressed capacity for clairaudience. Exercises which encourage you to speak and express your inner feelings and impressions will certainly aide you to develop your intuitive capacity for transmitting truth through words.

CLAIRVOYANCE

Clairvoyance, or clear seeing, is the intuitive ability to perceive truth in a visual framework. When intuition operates in this mode, we see visions, symbolic images, metaphorical pictures, and dreamlike sequences which have significant meaning when translated and interpreted.

Clairvoyance allows us to perceive subtle energies that exist beyond the perception of our physical eyes. This gift of inner vision allows us to see beyond the limits of physical matter, to perceive the subtle energetic structure of the physical universe, as well as the energies which exist between particles of physical matter. With our clairvoyance we can perceive the invisible and the visible, as well as that which connects structure and the void. Through clairvoyance, we can also see the patterns and rhythms existing in situations, people, relationships, and events. Looking into other people, we can see the path of their past experience and we can see their present state of being. We can perceive their behavioral patterns, emotional habits, and systems of beliefs.

Clairvoyance gives us the gift of artistic grace and the appreciation of form, flow, and color. The inner world of the imagination (initiation of images) is related to clairvoyant function, as are dreams, fantasy, and wishful thinking. If you possess a rich and flexible imagination and express artistic talent in a visual form, if you can perceive the deep underlying patterns of behavior in yourself and in others, and can see "behind" the actions of others, perceiving their needs and essential motivation, you are experiencing your capacity for clairvoyance.

If you find visualization techniques difficult, have problems remembering your dreams and using your imagination, and have a tendency to "not see things coming in your life," then this capacity is probably blocked in you. Difficulties with the eyes and tension headaches can also indicate suppression of your potential for inner vision.

Techniques which aid grounding, centering, and trusting will help you establish a basis within yourself from which you can begin to rediscover your capacity to see, both inwardly and in the external world. Exercises of visualization and those that insist on the capacities of detachment and witnessing will help you to find your true center and place more trust in your inner, intuitive perceptions.

KNOWINGNESS

This aspect of the intuition functions in a totally unique manner of direct perception. With our intuitive awareness, we suddenly know something to be true, to be as it is, and yet we may not perceive how we know that we know this truth. Knowingness functions beyond the other three pathways of intuitive expression in that we are faced with the challenge of simply trusting the information we receive as a truth, even though we do not receive other sensory, auditory, or visual evidence to support the information we are receiving. For this ability to function within us, we are required to take an internal "quantum leap" of both consciousness and self-trust. We must be willing to act on the guidance we receive in complete trust that the information is correct and in accordance with the truth of the situation we are investigating with our intuitive perception.

When we can allow ourselves to function at this level of intuitive perception, our lives become an ongoing, unfolding, creative experience of trust, communion, and a sense of belonging. At this level of expression, we realize that we are intrinsically linked to the creative intelligence of our universe and that we can participate in the expression of that intelligence.

When we experience our knowingness, we understand that, by our very nature, we are illuminated beings. All that exists, that has already existed, that will exist, is accessible to our conscious awareness at this level of perception. Time does not operate in the same linear mode that we are used to when we function through our rational, logical mind.

At this level of awareness, the concept of separation simply dissolves away and we are able to perceive the absolute perfection and chaotic order of the universe, as well as the way it is playfully unfolding and revealing its mystery to us. Intuitively, we both understand and accept the truth of our perceptions as we receive them, each insight arriving in relationship to the harmony of the whole. We realize that we are the creators of our concepts of reality, based on the framework of our attitudes and belief systems and that, therefore, we have the ability to transform these fundamental frameworks according to choice and free will.

It can be helpful and encouraging to be aware that we are all capable of functioning at this level of perception and personal intuitive awareness. It is our birthright and our natural state of being. Our intuitive self is waiting to guide us to this state.

CHAPTER THREE

Intuition Is a Catalyst for Personal Evolution

Intuition is our inner knowingness, the wisdom of our soul. When we know something with our intuition, it is a knowingness we feel in our bones, in our heart, a certainty that resonates throughout our entire body/being.

By learning to access the intuitive capacity innate within us we can access our own truth, as well as the truth of others. If we ask our intuition to show us the direction that is the most appropriate for us, if we ask to know the truth about a given situation, our intuition will provide the answers, indicating the most appropriate path for us to follow in relation to each situation we encounter in our lives.

Knowing the truth in a given moment and understanding the dynamics of a situation in which we find ourselves gives us certain advantages in our lives. But are we willing to act on the truth? Can we follow the truth we perceive, thanks to the perceptions of our intuitive self? If we do not follow the guidance we receive from our intuition, we will not reap the potential benefits offered by its counsel.

INTUITION AND RISK

Finding the courage to follow the guidance offered by your intuition can be a demanding challenge. Developing confidence and trust in your intuition takes time and requires personal commitment. Courage is a quality essential to intuition development, because you must be willing to take a risk—the risk that you may be wrong. The discovery that you have been wrong in an action or a decision is often difficult to accept and manage. However, if you do not take the risk, you will never know.

There is, in fact, a series of challenges we face in the development of the intuition. The first is getting in contact with the intuition. The second is learning how to live with it—how to share our intuition and be true to this aspect of ourselves in relationship to others. The third is gaining something through the existence of your intuition.

What do you have to gain by developing your intuition? Let us imagine that it has become imperative to you to begin to utilize your intuition. You are aware that this aspect of you has been dormant, sleeping. You have neglected your intuitive self terribly, but now you would like to wake up and begin to share this aspect of yourself in your world. What do you have to gain? You will not wake up unless there is a gain. This is normal. It is painful to wake up. It is easier to dream, to stay wrapped up in a comfortable, reassuring illusion. It is challenging to wake up, to become aware, to become conscious. What will you gain by developing your intuition?

INTUITION AND ENGAGEMENT

If you really make a commitment to your intuition, you will evolve more deeply and more thoroughly, and gain a greater lucidity about your process of personal evolution. You will develop to your potential more quickly. However, to transform and evolve is not necessarily an easy process. It is certainly easier to stay asleep than to wake up and take responsibility for yourself, your life, and the direction in which you are evolving. If, however, you are tired of sleeping, of being a victim, of feeling lost, out of control, and confused, then developing your intuition will serve you well. It will give you a resource to which you can always turn—a resource that is inside you and that is always there, waiting patiently to guide and serve you.

INTUITION AND CHOICE

The commitment you make to your intuitive self is a deep commitment. It is an engagement that will challenge you, both internally and externally, to become more honest, more authentic. At times, this commitment may throw your life into a state of temporary chaos. If you are truly well in your life, well on your chosen path, and aligned with your purpose, then your engagement to your intuition will simply improve your life even further, adding dimensions of richness and deepness to an already fulfilling path.

However, if you are not where you should be, where you could be—if you are not involved in a type of work that really suits you, if you are not satisfied with your intimate relationships and family life, if you feel lost and misplaced with yourself—then developing your intuition may very well push you so that changes begin to happen in your life. Change will begin because change is what you need. Your intuitive self wants you to be well—wants you to be in the right place, at the right time, with the right people. Your intuitive self will always guide you toward whatever is the most appropriate, the most perfect for you. However, your deep and true need may not be the same as your conditioned idea of what you need.

If this is the case, you will discover you have a problem. You will be challenged by your intuitive self to see, to feel, and to understand your problem more clearly. You will be challenged to solve the problem—to create concrete changes in your life. If, in your conditioned, programmed idea of yourself, you want one thing but your deepness needs something else, then you will have a decision to make. You will have a choice: should you follow the deep need or should you follow the desire? There is always a choice. There is always free will.

For example, if I want a hamburger for lunch, but the deep need of my body is for something simpler and nourishing, like a fresh salad, I can eat the hamburger and survive. I will not be punished for following my desire rather than my true need. I have the advantage of knowing my need, even if I do not follow it. Perhaps by following my desire, by fulfilling my desire, I will eventually go beyond it. The next time I face this same decision, I may choose the salad and nourish my deep need rather than my desire.

INTUITION AND TRUST

The more you listen to your inner guidance and follow its wisdom, the more you will trust that it brings you what is best for you. To discover that, however, you have to take the risk of following that guidance.

For example, you may have had a job for many years that you no longer enjoy. But the job pays you well. You ask your intuition for guidance and the response you receive is: "Leave this job. You are not nourished in your deepness by this work. You are not evolving. Be open to other possibilities." Your rational self will probably not be in agreement with this guidance. It may respond with: "But if I quit this job, what will I do? I've done this job for twenty years. I'm 45 years old. What else can I do? No job, no money; no money, no place; no place, no importance." Yet every time you ask the question, you receive the same response. "Leave the job . . . leave the job."

Sooner or later you will have to choose, you will have to reach a decision. Do you want to be comfortable in your life? Yes, of course! Do you want to explore, evolve? Yes, of course! Is it really your intuition guiding you to leave your work, or is it the neurotic fantasy of a bored mind, idling its hours away at the office desk? If you leave, what will happen? Will there be another job for you? Or will you eventually join the ranks of the unemployed, desperate and miserable, obliged to accept any job eventually offered to you?

This is the level of risk we are talking about with the development of the intuition. Real risks. Risks that can change your life. Not a choice between a hamburger and a salad, but a choice that can have an impact on your whole life. This is how the intuition can challenge you. Very often, too often, you are not where you really wish to be in your life. You are not satisfied with where you are and with the people who surround you, because you are not satisfied with yourself. You do not feel nourished in your deepness. Something essential is missing. This inner sense of lack, of loss, is a state experienced daily by many, many people.

INTUITION AND JOY

Something you can always count on with your intuition is that, when it guides you and you follow it, you will have more joy in your heart and you will experience more joy in your life. As a result of the changes you create, you will feel nourished in the deepness of your heart, so that when you finally make the decision to leave the job, you will feel a release, a relief. "I did it! I'm unemployed . . . and I feel good!" The release is something you feel in your deepness, a feeling of certainty and of rightness. However, you have to take the risk and do it to feel it. You have to act on the decision to have the result. Great courage is needed.

It is difficult to change. It is difficult to let go of the past. It is even more difficult to follow your own truth. Other people can become frightened, threatened, if you follow your own truth. If you take the risk to be true, real, and courageous, if you begin to follow your heart, other people's concept of their reality can become very threatened. Even if they love you, even if they want the best for you, even if they want to see you happy, joyful, and content, they are not going to encourage you to follow your heart because of their own fears, their own lack of courage, and their own unhappiness—not to mention their fear of losing you from their lives. Great courage is needed to listen to your intuitive guidance and follow the path of your heart.

INTUITION AND THE HEART

To succeed on the path of intuition you must have a warrior's spirit—courage, determination, and a profound belief in yourself. You must be willing to let go of all excess baggage in your life so you can go forward with lucidity and lightness. You must advance, even if you feel fear in your belly and dread in your mind. Once you choose this path, you cannot go back; you can only go onward. You can stop and rest, you can look back to the past with nostalgia, and you can delay your next step with the procrastinations of a weary mind, but you cannot go back. Why? Because your heart, your soul, your awakening, strengthening wisdom will not let you. It is as simple as that.

Even though, at times, the path of a warrior spirit is challenging, difficult, and tiring, the self-empowerment, personal lucidity, and self-reliance that result are worth the effort. There is nothing more enriching than the inner knowingness that you have found your path and you are walking it with the agreement and encouragement of your deepest self.

The path of the intuition is a path of the heart, a path of the soul. It is a path that leads you to yourself, that leads you home. In this homecoming, you can find true remembrance—remembrance of yourself, of your place, of your purpose. In this homecoming, you can rediscover the joy of your heart, the dance of your light being, and the ancient wisdom of your soul. You can know that you are not alone, that you were never abandoned. In forsaking yourself, in forgetting yourself, you lost your sense of yourself and so experienced abandonment. In coming home to yourself, to your intuitive heart, you nourish yourself in the deepest way possible. You accept responsibility for your own well-being and, in doing so, you liberate yourself from dependence on others. From a position of liberated independence you can begin to create personal relationships which are a true exchange, a true sharing, and a true joy to live.

CHAPTER FOUR

Intuition—the Forgotten Gift

Given the advantages we can experience through reconciliation with our intuitive self, it is surprising to consider that the vast majority of society goes through life without ever consciously taking the time to develop a relationship with this aspect of human experience. Preoccupied by the details of daily life, the demands of job, family, and existence in a material world, we have collectively relegated our inner world of soul, spirit, and being to a place of minor importance. We have lost our true identity. Tragically, we are no longer aware that something precious, an essential quality, has been lost to us.

Too often searching for security through material gain and worldly recognition, we have allowed our sense of values to become distorted. Our concepts of quality have been confused with those of quantity. Image has become more important than authenticity. We have become a people without purpose, without origins, and, therefore, without traditions to guide us on our way. The spiritual path, once recognized as a vocation which added value to the collective well-being of society, has been reduced, at the end of our 20th century, to an indulgence for the privileged few who can afford it, or else viewed as an escape for the marginal misfits who cannot find their way in a hard and competitive world. We have separated ourselves from nature, from the rhythm of the seasons, and from the very movement of the life-flow within our own bellies. We live our lives cut off from others, cut off even from ourselves, and we have lost an awareness of the mysteries that once belonged to us as a heritage of our incarnation.

Living, as we do, in a world full of fear, suffering, and sadness, we think it can be no other way. We cannot imagine a world united, a world at peace, a world in harmony with itself. We have, as a people, fallen far from a state of grace. The fall is reflected all around us, every day, in ways both large and small. We have lost our sense of community and fraternity. Others have become threats to us and we feel we must protect ourselves from their violence, separating ourselves, withdrawing. We have lost our sense of communion. We belong now only to ourselves and we are far from the God and nature to which we owe our origins.

We have lost our capacity to communicate and to offer with our words the gift of who we are. We can no longer share our hearts with others. So much has been lost, so much has been forsaken. In our urge to gain independence and express our individuality, we have made the collective mistake of cutting ourselves off from our roots, from our original source of nourishment. We have separated ourselves from our own hearts, from our own true being. Yet we wonder why we find the world so cruel, so hard, so lacking in heart and soul.

As a people, we face a collective crisis and we can only survive if we join together in integrity, fraternity, and authenticity. We must now come back to ourselves. We must reexamine our identities, our origins, and our destinies. We must contemplate why we have become so separated from ourselves, so cut off from others, so alienated from nature, from God, and from the Source. We must heal ourselves of our past traumas and create the possibility within ourselves for reconciliation—a reconciliation, above all, with our own being.

WHY IS INTUITION NONFUNCTIONAL?

When we consider intuition as a nonfunctional capacity, we face the image of a human being advancing through life without reference to depth or essential being. Given a restricted access to inner resources and qualities fundamental to well-being, as well as a lack of an essential inner integrity, it is no wonder that so many people suffer from chronic depression, sadness, and despair. The roots of human alienation, of separation from original nature and essential being, can perhaps be traced back to the mythological fall from the grace of God and the misadventures in the Garden of Eden. The well-intentioned but badly executed search for self-knowledge has led us farther and farther from the essential truth of ourselves. At the same time, since we have answered many questions about the structure and nature of the physical universe, there are evident advantages to the search for understanding embarked upon so long ago. We need not go back so far in time, however, to explore what caused us to become so alienated from our intuitive selves. We need only look at life and the traditions by which we live it in today's world to find an explanation for the terrible fragmentation of our inner potential and integrity.

THE BIRTH EXPERIENCE

For the majority of infants born into the modern world, birth is a violent experience.

The process of labor and childbirth has always been something of a physical trauma for both mother and child, but, in natural circumstances, a few days of rest and recuperation restore both mother and infant to normal physical, emotional, and psychological good health.

The natural stress of labor and childbirth is a stress that babies are equipped to manage. The atmosphere into which newborns are delivered, however, is all too often cold, clinical, and noisy. Babies, taken from their mothers, umbilical cords swiftly cut and tied, are obliged to breathe instantly, with no transition time to adapt their lungs to the cold air by which they are suddenly surrounded. Whisked away, they are suctioned, injected, washed, tagged, measured, and weighed. The lucky ones are then returned to their mothers for contact and a cuddle. For others, it may be hours before they find themselves returned to the safety and security of maternal arms.

The hospital is cold and noisy. The lights are bright. Babies are handled by people they don't yet know. They are sensitive, vulnerable, innocent, fresh, and new to this world. They cannot speak, but that does not mean they are not aware. They are helpless, but that does not mean they cannot feel.

In fact, babies feel everything that is happening to them. They hear every noise, every word that is spoken. They may not understand, but that does not mean they do not experience. Too often they are born, in all their precious beauty and sensitivity to this world, only to be treated on arrival as insensitive objects, unaware of the environment. Newborns are not recognized as the beings that they are. They are not acknowledged as beings with sensitivity and intelligence, as souls with stories. They are not recognized for who they are beyond their newborn bodies. For this reason, the suffering in their beings will be terrible.

It is only because of the environment they are born into, because of the quality of welcome the babies receive, that birth is experienced as something violent. If, in the first precious hours of life, the being of each newborn is not recognized, acknowledged, and nourished, how can we expect the child to harbor this aspect of self intact? If we do not recognize the being in children and help them to maintain this essential and integral reference to themselves, they will surely forget who they are, as we have forgotten and as our parents have forgotten before us.

THE BODY, RESPIRATION, AND
ENERGETIC BLOCKAGES

The way we come into this world is indelibly marked on us and within us. Many human beings never fully recover from the original trauma of their birth experience. Birth by violence, with instrumental intervention, into an environment that seems hostile and full of overwhelmingly new sensations, creates fear and even terror in the newborn. Infants breathe, but they breathe in fear. They breathe instinctively, for life, but they feel threatened and in a state of panic. They are frightened and overwhelmed and do not easily find the reassurance needed to calm them. Their sole point of reference, in the beginning, is the mother. If they can bond with the mother, if the mother can hold and nurse them, they will become secure and begin to recover from the birth trauma. If the mother is not available and cannot provide the comfort and security needed to relax and breathe naturally, the child will retreat into the trauma, which will remain on an unconscious level throughout life.

This trauma will influence babies' respiration, their emotional nature, and their psychological structure. The fear experienced in the first few hours of life will determine the future relationships they establish with their bodies, their breath, and their external environment. If the fear is not resolved and integrated, they will establish an instinctive fear-reflex toward life. Their breathing will be too shallow and too hurried—a stressed breath. They will become nervous, hypersensitive, and tense. Due to this state of inner tension, the circulatory systems of the body will have difficulty functioning efficiently, and they will not receive the physical and energetic nourishment they need to develop fundamental physical health and psychological well-being.

Lacking a basis of psychological security, it will be difficult for individuals to develop trust in themselves, in others, in life, and in existence. It will be difficult to relax, to let go. It will be almost impossible to imagine life as a process of gentle unfolding, as a journey of evolution. The external world will not seem friendly and welcoming. It will seem, rather, something to protect oneself against. A protective, defensive posture will be established in the physical body which will result in further physical and energetic blockages. A full and flowing respiration will be difficult to attain, thus causing a sense of alienation and separation from the physical body. Robbed of a sense of physical well-being, these individuals will find it virtually impossible to establish a sense of spiritual harmony and equilibrium.

FAMILY—TRADITIONS, CONDITIONING, EXPECTATIONS

We are subjected from birth to a whole host of parental expectations, projections, and behavioral programmings that influence both our social development and our fundamental sense of ourselves. We are molded by the ideas of our parents; we unconsciously conform to their expectations of us, behaving as they wish and accepting the limits they impose upon us. We are raised to perceive the world through their eyes and in relation to their personal experience. Very often, during adolescence in particular, we feel we must fight against the family to gain the right to discover, explore, and assume our proper originality. We are obliged to reject the traditional male/female stereotypes imposed by social conditioning in order to discover who we really are, to move beyond the definition given to us by the sex of the body into which we are born.

Regardless of their good intentions, our parents often make us feel imprisoned within their value system. Regardless of their love for us, they limit us by their conceptions of who we are and what we are capable of. If we stay within the confines of family traditions, we have a tendency to unconsciously reproduce the lives of our parents. Adhering to the standards expected of us, we maintain a certain security. By making this choice, however, we do not give ourselves the opportunity to discover our true potential and then develop it.

LIFE STYLE

We are not taught to give importance to our spiritual well-being. Nor are we taught how to nourish our relationship with nature and light. From a very early age, we are conditioned to search outside ourselves for nourishment, entertainment, attention, and exchange. We are not taught to reflect, contemplate, and meditate. We are not told that we can find the answers to our questions within ourselves, in the stillness of our deeper being.

Our lives are organized in such a way that we do not find the time to take care of ourselves. We take care of the family, of work, of the house. Afterward, too often, there is no time left for other things. At the end of the day, we fall to sleep exhausted and the next morning, we begin again. We do not find the time to prepare nourishment that is balanced and wholesome and so we become tired, drained, and discouraged. We are stressed. There are too many details to attend to, too much noise, too much violence and abuse. We cannot breathe. We need to renew ourselves in nature, but we do not have the time, because there are too many other important and pressing things we must take care of first. We are caught in the trap of "doing" and "having"—and we are all caught in it together. We do not give ourselves the right to experience being and so the circle of stress continues to turn and we turn with it, trapped and going nowhere.

RATIONAL MIND AND BELIEF SYSTEMS

We do not find the answers we seek by thinking. Thinking is another series of circles bringing us back to our point of departure. Because of our dependence on the rational, logical mind and our belief that it is the only mind in which we can have confidence for solving problems and arriving at solutions, we propel ourselves deeper and deeper into despair. We have been collectively conditioned to give priority to the logical mind in all matters. We were trained for hours and hours at school to be rational and logical. We were taught to use our rational minds and to believe in logic, evidence, and scientific reasoning. We were conditioned to neglect the creative hemisphere of our brain. We were punished for "daydreaming," for relaxing our concentration and allowing our imaginations to function. We were taught to believe that our personal value to society was largely determined by our scholastic capacity.

Between the pressures of school and the conditioning of the family, by the time we reach puberty, we have been programmed to accept belief systems about ourselves from which we will probably never escape as long as we live. Educated, socialized, and then integrated into the system of modern daily life, we live our lives the best that we can, using whatever resources we can find within us to help us through the difficult periods of questions, doubts, and mental depression.

RELIGION AND TRADITIONAL ARCHETYPES

Many of us are without religion, not because we were not born to it, but because the religion we were born to has not satisfied our criteria for what we feel religious experience should or could be. The Christian God, whether Catholic or Protestant, Anglican or Methodist, can hardly be considered a readily accessible God. If we follow the teachings of our churches, we must submit to the mediation of priests in order to have access to His presence, guidance, and wisdom.

The interpretations given to the teachings of Christ by the church have taught that we, as a people, are impure, tarnished, sinners by our very human nature. They teach that the physical body and our desire for pleasure are devilish temptations, taking us away from God and leading our souls to certain peril. If we believe what we have been taught by religion, there is little, if any, hope for us at all. The belief that we are imperfect and damned to exile from God's love because of our imperfection is deeply ingrained in those who have been touched by the Christian religion. Regardless of all that we may do or try to be, we will probably never arrive at the perfect purity demanded of us by our stern and judgmental Father.

In our churches, we are encouraged to pray and taught to trust in a higher good, in justice, and in mercy. We are guided to develop faith in the love of God. We are given values that help us to live in harmony, respect, and cooperation with our fellow human beings. We are taught about the importance of community spirit. We are reminded that God exists regardless of how far from Him we may have strayed.

But we are no longer taught that God and the Divine Spirit also exist within us. We are not encouraged to search for our God in nature. We are not encouraged to believe that, from a place of inner silence, in the deepness of our heart, we can speak with God and receive His love and healing for ourselves whenever we may need it. So, disappointed, we have turned away from religion. We do not close our eyes to pray; we do not meditate in the presence of our God.

NEGLIGENCE

We cannot say that any one person in particular is responsible for the state of neglect into which our spiritual well-being has fallen. It is difficult to debate with any certainty that the level of spiritual consciousness of our society is worse now than it was one, or two hundred, or even two thousand years ago. Certainly, we cannot reasonably hold our parents, our teachers, or our obstetricians responsible for the fact that we cannot organize our lives in a manner that will ensure our ongoing personal and spiritual evolution. At the same time, accepting

all the responsibility on our own shoulders seems equally unreasonable and unnecessarily guilt-provoking.

It is as though we have all fallen into a long and deep sleep of collective forgetfulness. From this sleepy fog, it is extremely difficult to
regain consciousness. The neglectful habits we have developed
belong to all of us and so they do not seem to be habits at all, but
rather the normal way of life of our day and age.

INTUITION AND THE
TURN OF THE MILLENNIUM

For all its tragedy and woe, our world remains a place full of hope
and possibility. We have the mixed fortune of living in an epoch that
is particularly fraught with mortal danger and, at the same time,
bursting with evolutionary breakthroughs on the levels of human
consciousness, scientific revelation, and global political negotiation
and reconciliation.

The turn of a millennium is a time of endings, of completion. It
is also a time of new beginnings. Collectively, humanity is facing a
symbolic death, a death that will be followed naturally by rebirth.
Individually, we are experiencing a process of alchemical transformation in our inner worlds of thought and feeling. As our century
draws to a close, we are faced with the possibility of accelerated
personal evolution. There is a "quickening" occurring in the global
consciousness of humanity that signifies the long-awaited arrival of
the Age of Aquarius, the New Age. Perhaps it is not arriving as we
might have imagined it, but it is arriving nonetheless. We are all present and being whisked along by its coming. The effects of the accel-
eration are felt most strongly in our inner world, in the world of our
consciousness. It is an epoch for insights, for revelations, and for
breakthroughs. We are being offered the possibility of liberating
ourselves from illusion, limitation, and unnecessary suffering. We
find ourselves faced with the choice of greater individual freedom.

Reconciliation within ourselves and with our loved ones becomes an imperative rather than a preference. Internally we are transforming. We are becoming more sensitive, more perceptive. Our scale of values is shifting. We are searching for the meaning of quality and trying to rediscover our lost integrity. There is hope for our humanity. We are beginning to understand the meaning of responsibility, of fraternity, and of integrity.

Thanks to the epoch of which we are all a part, humanity will eventually give birth to a new philosophy of life. Within that philosophical framework, intuition will have a place of importance, a place of value, and a place of respect. Individuals will be encouraged to develop their intuition, to listen to their feelings, to follow their inner guidance. The capacity of each person to access and trust their inner truth will be integrated into the developmental programs of education from the earliest age. The being, with all its qualities and inner resources, will again find its place in the world.

2

THE DIMENSION OF BODY,
MIND, AND BEING:
UNDERSTANDING AND
TRANSFORMING
OUR INNER WORLD

CHAPTER FIVE

The Body—Temple of the Soul

The physical body is the means through which we accomplish the purpose of our lives, as well as the physical anchor that holds us to this Earth. At times, we may feel restricted by the limitations of the physical body and burdened by the density of physical matter within which our consciousness is contained. We may yearn to be free, to fly, to escape the confines of these far-from-perfect bodies in which we find ourselves—bodies which age, wrinkle, grow flabby, fat, thin, and which do not seem to stand the tests of time and gravity with any grace at all.

Be that as it may, the body we have is nonetheless an impressive instrument by any standards. If we stop to consider how we subject our bodies to a lifetime of wear and tear, we can only be grateful for its tenacity and loyalty. Take a moment to think about how many miles your feet have walked for you, how many images your eyes have seen, how many meals your teeth have chewed. Think about all the actions your hands have executed for you—all you have touched, held, carried, dropped, and pushed away. Imagine all the hair your head has grown for you, all the breaths your lungs have taken. Think for a moment of your heart, beating endlessly for you, sustaining your life even as you sleep and dream.

We are all guilty of taking our bodies for granted at one time or another, and on one level or another. Most of us are quite ignorant about the physiological functioning of the body, leaving that domain of knowledge and understanding to doctors. It is only when we become ill and are in pain that we begin to think of our bodies, only because of the discomfort of sickness that we accept the obligation to change our physical and nutritional habits. It is a sad fact that suffering is very often the catalyst for awareness and change. Suffering obliges us to pay attention, to listen, and to act differently in relationship to the functioning of the physical body. Pain demands attention and disease must be treated successfully if we are to survive and thrive into old age.

Many of us are terribly dissociated from our bodies, having never really accepted responsibility for our physical well-being beyond the basic maintenance necessary to "keep on going." We ignore our bodies, neglect them, abuse them, and take them for granted. Then we wonder why we feel cut off from ourselves, out of touch, unattractive, and lacking in vitality.

In the philosophical framework of the intuitive teachings, the body is considered a sacred instrument. As conscious beings with a purpose to realize, the physical body is a sacred temple, the sacred space through which we function, through which we express who we are, and to which we come home to rest and recuperate. The body is recognized as something divine, an essentially spiritual creation, for which we are responsible for the duration of earthly life. If we wish to realize the potential of our being through creative expression and a meaningful contribution to life, we must honor and respect the vehicle through which the realization is possible.

To develop the intuition, we must acknowledge the place of the physical body and its importance in relation to our path through life. It is through the body that our intuition functions and that our inner senses perceive the reality of existence all around us. The less healthy, balanced, and physically nourished we are, the more our perception of the external world will be distorted due to our unbalanced physical state. Because body and mind are intrinsically related, physical dis-ease reflects mental imbalance, just as mental extremes find their reflection through emotional imbalance.

In paying attention to the well-being of the physical body, we begin to assume responsibility for our spiritual evolution. The physical body is tangible, a reflection of concrete reality. It therefore provides us with concrete feedback about ourselves and our state of well-being, on both a physical and a more subtle level of being. It is not difficult to take care of our physical well-being. With a moderate dose of common sense, we can note the essentials we need to provide a basis of health for our bodies.

1. Balanced nutrition
2. Light
3. Fresh air
4. Exercise
5. Rest and relaxation

To live a healthy life, we simply need to remember the wisdom of the saying: "All things in moderation." We can eat well, preparing the maximum of fresh foods possible and avoiding processed products, limiting our intake of meat and dairy foods, concentrating on fruits, vegetables, and cereals as our primary food sources. Eating in moderation, we are assured of efficient digestion and elimination. Choosing foods that are simple, clean, and vital will transform our bodies into clean and vital instruments.

The physical body needs to breathe and move, to exercise. We must honor its needs if it is to function efficiently for us. Regular outdoor activity is essential to good health. Stretching, breathing, walking, dancing—any aerobic activity practiced regularly—ensures physical well-being. We also need to relax. Periods of meditation, resting, sleeping, and just being are necessary so that the body can function at its optimum potential.

To honor the body we must give it attention and we must respect it. Attention to hygiene, diet, exercise, rest, and relaxation are practical ways through which we can assume responsibility for our physical incarnation, thus assuring physical well-being as well as spiritual evolution.

By remembering that our bodies are sacred temples, we can attend to its maintenance with respect and sensitivity. We can be kind to our bodies by being kind to ourselves. Accepting the limitations of our bodies, we accept ourselves with our limitations. Training the body to go further, to go beyond old limits, we encourage ourselves to take risks and go beyond old habits. Listening to the needs of the body, we listen to ourselves and respond to our essential needs, thus assuming the role of self-healer.

CHAPTER SIX

The Physiology of Fear and Trust

When developing the intuition, we are focusing on developing sensitivity and attunement to the profound and subtle energy flows occurring around us in both our external environment and within our physical and energetic bodies.

The five senses of the physical body—touching, tasting, hearing, smelling, and seeing—are the information gatherers for the brain. They are its antennae. The brain, though situated within the skull, is connected to the entire physical body through a complex system of nerves which never cease relaying information back to the brain.

The mind, conscious awareness, exists throughout the entire body, within every cell of the body. Every second, huge amounts of sensory information are gathered by the five primary senses and travel to a section of the brain known as the hypothalamus. The hypothalamus is like a vast, centralized computer. It analyzes and deciphers the information it receives and decides what to do with the sensory input it has sorted.

Some information is sent to the section of your brain that brings sensory input to your conscious awareness. For example, if you put your hand on a hot stove, you get a message, very quickly and very consciously, to remove your hand from the heat. However, most of the information (approximately 95 percent) is transferred to your unconscious mind. Your physical body responds physiologically to this sensory input, often without registering on a conscious level. If your brain receives sensory information it considers threatening to your well-being, it directs the hypothalamus to alert the pituitary gland (the master gland of the body). This gland directs the adrenal glands to secrete hormones (glandular substances) that help your body cope with the threatening situation by fighting, running away, or freezing (becoming paralyzed by fear). This function is known as the "fight or flight" mechanism. Its purpose is simply to ensure your survival in life-threatening situations. When the fight or flight mechanism is activated, other body functions are temporarily suppressed. Once the threatening situation has been resolved, normal physiological balance is restored.

The hypothalamus cannot readily discern the difference between a real threat, a remembered threat, or an imagined possible future threat to your life. Close your eyes and imagine you are precariously balanced on the outside windowledge of a building, on the twelfth floor. The window is closed; the ledge is narrow; the wind is gusty and blowing hard. Your body will physiologically adapt itself to protect you from possible death. This happens even though, in reality, you are sitting in a comfortable armchair imagining this scenario in your mind. What is perceived by an individual in life as threatening depends largely on cultural and family conditioning, as well as on personal life experience. If a person thinks a situation is threatening, it becomes threatening in his or her imagination and the body reacts accordingly.

Only a limited amount of information can be stored and accessed in the conscious mind at one time, so most of the memories and accumulated experiences of life are stored in the unconscious mind. The hypothalamus refers to this accumulated experience stored in its computer banks in order to decide how to direct the body to respond to any given situation. The directions it gives depend largely on the habitual reactions you have programmed in your brain.

A habit is simply the same decision made over and over again. You have learned to survive many threatening situations in your life, so this process has functioned successfully for you on many occasions. However, there are many instances when a habitual reaction is, in fact, not the most useful choice in a situation, or the one apt to bring about the best possible outcome. If you are habitually fearful, anxious, or threatened—on a conscious or unconscious level, either by real or imagined situations—the fight or flight mechanism will be triggered in your body and your sensory input channels will be temporarily suppressed. If your senses are not gathering information reliably, you cannot accurately perceive what is happening around you, because, at that moment, you are preoccupied with survival issues and are not at all concerned with subtle exterior events occurring within your vicinity.

Your intuition relies on the balanced and regular functioning of your senses to operate and bring you conscious awareness of events occurring around and within you. If you are in a state of fear, if your body/mind is tense and unreceptive because you are engaged in the survival tactics of fighting, freezing, or fleeing, your intuition cannot function. The intuition can only be fully functional when you are relaxed—when you feel safe, secure, and trusting of the environment surrounding you. When you feel safe, the muscular system of the body can relax and the mind (awareness) can operate in a state of relaxed alertness. When you are relaxed, the body functions in a state of homeostasis, a state of balance. When you are in a state of balance within yourself, you naturally feel safe and secure. When you feel safe, you can allow yourself to be vulnerable, available, and open to your internal and external environments.

In intuition development, it is essential to learn to relax and be available, so that your intuition can begin to function for you. Habitual fear-reaction patterns must be addressed, diffused, and resolved, so that an inner state of relaxed alertness becomes a preferred habitual way of life.

Intuition development teaches breathing, grounding, and centering techniques you can use in daily life to maintain a state of relaxed awareness. In this state, your senses can be fully open to receive the complete range of sensory information occurring all around you. When you feel clearly, hear clearly, and see clearly, you will naturally maintain a greater equilibrium in yourself and in your interactions with others.

Gaining control over the chronic activation of the fight or flight mechanism of the body requires self-monitoring and an awareness of inner thought patterns and habits. Self-awareness is an acquired habit, developed over time by personal choice and self-investigation. To be self-aware, you must be willing to be honest with yourself and accept responsibility for your own personal growth. From a position of personal responsibility, it is possible to assume full creative control of your health, your state of mind, and your sense of well-being.

Your intuition is a subtle, delicate, and very powerful aspect of your being that requires a very specific environment in which to function optimally. Your physical body is the environment through which the intuition integrates your experiences in life. For this reason, the state of the body/mind must be fully addressed and transformed for you to obtain the best results from developing your intuition.

CHAPTER SEVEN

Breath, Movement, and Emotion

All our physical problems and illnesses are signs of disharmony within ourselves, signs of certain qualities of energy misunderstood and incorrectly utilized in our lives. Our health problems exist in relationship to our attitudes and belief systems—in particular those beliefs which we have acquired from our experience of life, from our past. The belief systems to which we adhere often create situations in our lives where we find ourselves in emotional states of conflict, confusion, and inner turmoil.

Perturbing emotions that we experience in these situations are reflections of the conflict between the movement of our essential life-force energy and our belief systems. Emotional reactions are manifestations of the "internal friction" caused by the movement of our inner being meeting the resistance of our mental attitudes. The inner battle caused by the meeting of these two forces creates emotional as well as energetic tension and has a powerful effect on the physical body and respiratory patterns.

Inner conflict reflects throughout the body, causing muscular tension, pain, and, at times, physical illness. These symptoms are often transitory in nature, shifting and changing according to the nature of the belief system with which we are "doing battle." Despite their transitory nature, the symptoms of inner conflict that we experience both physically and emotionally are powerful and often very disturbing.

As we align ourselves more and more with our intuitive self and thus with our inner being and soul, we pass through a transition in which we experience a vast range of different emotional states existing within our inner world. Entering into a more authentic contact with the emotional aspect of ourselves, we encounter a veritable ocean of feelings—waves of sadness and joy, anger and fear, despair and hope, regret and forgiveness. Our emotional state can change radically from day to day, moment to moment. We experience extremes of feelings, both negative and positive. Even though these extremes may be difficult to manage, we feel alive, awakened, and empowered by the sheer intensity of our inner emotional movement.

At times, we may feel overwhelmed by the volume of emotions we encounter. Even though our goal is the realignment and centering of our intuitive self, it seems that just the opposite is occurring. We are becoming lost and disoriented in a movement we cannot seem to follow or manage. It is important to remember in these difficult moments that what we are experiencing is a passage, a period of inner alchemy that is necessary to the process of transformation in which we have engaged. After the storm, we will rediscover the calm. In accepting the waves of changing emotion as they come and go, we progressively learn to maintain a state of inner calm within our deepness, thus developing detachment from emotional extremes and realignment within our true center.

THE VALUE OF INDIVIDUAL SESSIONS

When we engage in a personal work of meditation and begin to realign our energies and our inner awareness, the tensions created by the meeting of our inner movement with mind are intensified for a certain period of time. An enormous amount of psychological material related to past experiences and belief systems begins to circulate within us and rises to the surface of our conscious awareness. We are faced with the possibility of a deep and thorough inner cleansing of our attitudes and habitual reactions, as well as a passage of physical purification and realignment.

Face to face with our inner world of thoughts and feelings, confronted by the demons and dragons of our shadow-self, it is difficult to distinguish between fact and fantasy, truth and illusion. Searching to establish reference points by which we can build a new and more appropriate life, we feel alienated from loved ones, alone in our inner research and questing.

Numerous advantages can accrue during a period of intense transition by engaging in personal work, one-on-one, with a health practitioner trained in psychotherapeutic techniques. Individual sessions create an atmosphere of support and guidance and the sense of being accompanied along the path. A professional relationship of confidentiality encourages exploration of deep inner states and honest communication in an accepting and nonjudgmental environment. Long-repressed emotional material can be expressed in a neutral environment, away from loved ones who, in moments of emotional turbulence when they can feel implicated, are more prone to react than simply listen.

BODYWORK AS A PSYCHOTHERAPEUTIC TOOL

During a period of intensive personal transformation, it is useful to receive regular sessions of bodywork (massage), to benefit fully from the inner changes which are occurring. Massage sessions help to realign the physical body and act directly on muscular and energetic tensions, liberating the respiration and encouraging circulation of the body's energetic systems. The healing power of touch and the personal physical contact generated by the "hands on" approach of massage encourage the development of a new awareness of the physical body and its relation to the emotional and mental states of being. With the assistance of a trained bodyworker, emotional traumas related to physical tension can be addressed, explored, released, and integrated.

The benefits experienced from a series of massage treatments include physical rebalancing and harmonization, deep and lasting relaxation, and a resolution to chronic inner conflict. Massage teaches us to accept our bodies, to listen to and respect the instinctive and intelligent guidance our bodies offer to us. The therapeutic quality of touch discovered in massage work creates physical and emotional healing and helps to reestablish trust in life, in self, and in others.

RESPIRATION AS A TRANSFORMATIONAL CATALYST

The power of the breath as a transformational catalyst has been recognized and utilized in many cultures since antiquity. Kriya Yoga, a traditional discipline of the East Indians, recognizes the breath as a vital instrument of internal purification and an essential tool for mastering of the physical and psychological body. In fact, the majority of meditation techniques proposed throughout the world recognize the role of respiration in relationship to the alteration of internal states of awareness.

The significance of breath and its value as a therapeutic tool in contemporary psychological practice has been advocated in several schools of body/mind therapy—Primal Therapy, Reichian Work, Postural Integration, Feldenkrais, Bio-energetics, and Rebirthing. Each of these modern schools holds its unique viewpoint and practices according to a specific method, yet each acknowledges the importance of the breath in the transformational process.

REBIRTHING (INTEGRATIVE BREATHWORK)

Rebirthing is a unique school of psychotherapy, named and developed by Leonard Orr in the United States in the early 1970s. Essentially simple and holistic in its philosophy, Rebirthing utilizes respiration as a primary catalyst for the creation of inner movement and evolution within the individual.

In the developmental phases of Rebirthing research, breathing sessions were largely oriented toward the reexperience of the actual birth process. Thus the name, Rebirthing. It was discovered during the early days of research that many individuals, especially those born in hospitals by modern obstetric procedures, had developed deep and fundamental fears in relation to life as a result of trauma at birth. The long-term effects of these deep and often largely suppressed fears included hypo-ventilation, social maladjustment, and chronic stress. When the trauma of birth was reexperienced and released, tremendous energy was also released and liberated throughout the entire body. Habitual breathing patterns underwent permanent transformation and physical symptoms of stress often disappeared entirely. Early researchers rebirthed thousands of people with consistent similar results.

It became evident that the experience of birth has a tremendous impact on unconsciously held belief systems about life itself and that belief systems play a significant role in the individual's interpretation and assimilation of life experiences.

BREATH AND BELIEF SYSTEMS

As the process of Rebirthing evolved over time, its focus shifted from the birth experience toward research on the potential of the breath in relationship to belief systems. Rebirthers began to explore the possibilities of personal transformation available by combining specific breathing methods with the power of focused affirmative thoughts.

Leonard Orr changed the name of Rebirthing to Conscious Connected Breathing. Rebirthing is also known around the world as Breath Therapy, Breathwork, and Breath Integration. As the process has evolved, so has the understanding of its potential. But the name

Rebirthing remains the most well-known term applied to this school of psychotherapy.

Essentially, Rebirthing recognizes the breath as the most simple, natural, and powerful inner resource available for creating an alteration in the state of being of an individual. Rebirthing begins as a physical experience, demanding full and continuous breathing over a specific period of time. Relaxing and breathing in a circular rhythm, the client maintains a focused awareness of sensations, emotions, thoughts, and memories as they come and go, experiencing and accepting these different phenomena without judgment or interpretation. Encouraged to relax, to accept, and to "let go," the client develops an awareness about their inner world of being, experiencing thoughts and emotions from a different perspective, progressively creating a new dynamic in the breathing process.

BLISS IS OUR BIRTHRIGHT

Surrounding the physical respiratory aspect of Rebirthing, we find a philosophy encouraging personal growth and spiritual transformation through self-understanding and acceptance. Rebirthing recognizes that the body, mind, and spirit are essentially connected and that change in the state of one aspect triggers change in the others. As a natural therapy, Rebirthing supports the view that individuals contain within themselves all the resources they need to develop to their full creative and spiritual potential. Furthermore, Rebirthing advocates that the essential state of being of the individual is one of bliss and a profound sense of well-being. Therefore, any experience other than bliss is the result of suppressed fear and emotional trauma due to past experience as yet unresolved by the individual.

THE PATH OF HEALING

When the client breathes, relaxes, and maintains awareness with an attitude of acceptance, an internal atmosphere is created which allows suppressed "material" to rise to the surface of awareness. Thoughts and memories which come to conscious awareness also have an emotional counterpart and a physical reference point in the body. As material surfaces and circulates in the body/mind, physical tension is affected and eventually dissolved, emotions are experienced and expressed, and insights occur. As physical and emotional release arrives, the breath deepens, flowing more fully and spontaneously. The client resolves and integrates past experiences, thereby progressively liberating the body/mind from past traumas and welcoming a respiration that circulates with greater freedom and ease.

LIBERATION

For many clients of Rebirthing, the breath work opens up a spiritual dimension of experience that has never before been encountered. At a certain moment, often following a significant passage of release and integration, the breath becomes completely liberated. In this moment, it is as though the body rediscovers how to breathe naturally and effortlessly. A barrier dissolves and the concept of self transforms, opening into a vast dimension of energy, light, and illumination. In this state, one is "in the light" and "is the light." The experience of breathing in light creates a state of inner ecstasy, profound relaxation, healing, and integration. The resulting sense of inner peace, reconciliation, and harmony can be carried into daily life with long-lasting results.

INTEGRATION

Encouraged to accept personal responsibility for their state of well-being and to adopt the principles of Rebirthing philosophy and practice into daily life, clients find themselves permanently transformed. Empowered both physically and spiritually, individuals find themselves more free to express their creativity, more able to adapt to the movement of life, and more available to participate in the creation of their path of choice.

Essentially, Rebirthing is a simple process—as simple as breathing. But the art of Rebirthing is subtle, delicate, and profound, a technique that must be learned and mastered to fully benefit from the transformation offered by its regular practice. As a pathway for spiritual transformation it holds great potential. As a means of exploring, expressing, and integrating emotional experience, it is unsurpassed in its proven efficiency and long-term results.

SELF-ACCEPTANCE AND INTUITION

Whether we like it or not, emotions are here to stay. Part of the body/mind mystery, feelings exist because we are incarnated, because we are alive. All attempts to control, negate, and repress emotional states result in physical symptoms of pain and illness. If we distance ourselves from our inner emotional world, we distance ourselves from our deepness, thus losing contact with our intuition.

Acceptance of the huge range of emotional states which occurs within us leads us, paradoxical though it may seem, to the development of a quality of healthy detachment toward our feelings. Practicing the principle of acceptance, we learn that we can experience the inner movement of our emotions as they circulate, recognizing their coming, their expression, and their departure, without becoming attached and overidentified with them. Developing the capacity of "inner witness," we learn to stay centered in front of all of our emotional states, no longer losing ourselves to them and, at the same time, respecting the power of their presence and the potential they offer us for self-expression. Giving permission to the existence of our emotions, we allow our inner movement to take form and flow. Aligned to the soul, emotions lead us to the heart, to the source of ourselves. Accepting the power of our feelings, we accept ourselves. And in self-acceptance, we are sure to find our healing path of transformation, evolution, and personal truth.

CHAPTER EIGHT

Belief Systems

A belief system can be defined as a series of ideas that we hold to be true based on personal experience and that have been tested sufficiently to be considered viable. We base our conceptions of the nature of reality on these systems.

THOUGHT IS CREATIVE

From the very first moments of life, the biocomputer of the body/mind begins to amass, identify, and classify data pertaining to the events occurring in our surrounding environment. Experiential data provides the framework through which belief systems are developed, tested, and verified.

Firsthand experience of life and the integration of that experience teaches us the survival skills we need to learn to be able to find our way through life. Our ideas of who we are and of what we are capable of achieving are based largely on firsthand experience, as well as information we have gathered from our parents and other family members during our early childhood. As beings, we may be conceived and born with unlimited potential and an open consciousness, but the process of socialization to which we are all necessarily subjected as infants very quickly begins to define our limits, spatially as well as behaviorally. Well before we begin to walk and talk, we have an established place in the family hierarchy—personality traits and idiosyncrasies, ancestral strengths and weaknesses, a gender advantage or disadvantage, and a host of other sociopsychological influences to which we have been exposed and to which we have unconsciously responded.

From the very beginning of our lives, we are taught to believe that we are a certain person, with a particular name and a personality to match, who will be capable of achieving or not achieving certain goals and aspirations. Depending on the social milieu into which we are born, the limitations we face will be more or less severe, and our chances of succeeding to become someone with whom we can be satisfied will be largely determined by the conditioning we have undergone.

Given that a large majority of human beings do not really believe in themselves and are not aware of themselves as a being with the creative power to shape and transform their world, most people do not believe that it is possible to change. Parents in our world do not often teach their children about the power of their minds, nor do they teach them about their light nature, their healing capacities, and their intuitive gifts. Thanks to parents, children are educated to respect the behavioral limits so necessary to the functioning of family and society.

Thanks to education, we are taught to use the intellectual capacity of our minds to think, read, write, and analyze. However, most of us have never been taught about the creative power of the mind. We have never heard our parents discuss the philosophy that thought is creative. It is only once we are adults, functioning as independent members of society, that we really begin to become aware of how many of our behaviors, habits and attitudes are inherited from our parents, and that these habits can be destructive and cause suffering, both to ourselves and to others.

When we begin to pay attention to our behavior, we observe that we react rather than respond to situations. We often sabotage ourselves from having what we really need and want. We often seem to act according to a type of "automatic pilot" behavior. Without thinking, we speak; without reflecting, we act; without looking, we assume to see; without listening, we reply. Many people spend their entire lives being the person they think they should be, without ever really asking themselves the question: "Who am I?"; without ever asking the question: "What do I need?"; without ever asking themselves: "Where am I going?"

When we begin to pay attention to our habitual behavior, we quickly discover that we cause ourselves great suffering, very often for no discernible reason. We often have ideas about ourselves which are negative and limiting. We have these same ideas about others and about life.

The ideas, attitudes, and belief systems we hold form a type of selective criteria or filter, through which we perceive and experience reality. The experiences we have confirm to us that our attitudes are correct, and so our belief systems are verified and reinforced. Unfortunately, many of the beliefs do not really serve us and can, in fact, be harmful to our well-being and peace of mind.

Belief systems inherited from the family or developed when we are youngsters, do not have a true value for us now, even though they continue to function through our habitual behavior and form an intrinsic part of our social personality. Because thoughts are essentially creative, we continue unconsciously to give life to our belief systems, regardless of whether or not they are ultimately useful.

By developing our intuition, we begin to pay attention to the quality of the thoughts we have, both on a conscious and an unconscious level. By accepting the possibility that thought is creative, we naturally begin to explore the thoughts that we hold within ourselves—thoughts about who we are, thoughts about others, and thoughts about the nature of life, of reality, of evolution, and of spiritual development. In exploring the quality of our belief systems and mental attitudes, we begin to identify beliefs which are ancestral, familial, social, and personal. With growing lucidity and discernment, we transform inherited belief systems that cause low self-esteem, failure, fear, and mistrust, replacing them with preferred attitudes of self-acceptance, encouragement, and trust. Learning to differentiate between our essential selves and our personalities, we let go of habitual behavior patterns that restrain us from being ourselves and adopt inner attitudes that encourage the expression of our innate creativity and talents.

CHAPTER NINE

The Personal Lie and the Eternal Key

The transformation of belief systems is a personal healing work that is both simple and profound. While the fundamental concepts are simple, the application of these concepts is a subtle process, demanding both skill and guidance. Unconscious fears can easily impede the successful discovery and transformation of self-limiting belief systems. It is important, therefore, that, when you decide to explore the exercises proposed in this chapter, you create a quiet time and place where you will be undisturbed for the duration of the exercises.

The practical exercises of the Personal Lie and the Eternal Key are designed to help you explore your belief systems, so that you can clarify the self-limiting ideas you hold on an unconscious level and liberate yourself from them. The steps of the belief-system process are designed to be followed with a friend. In a mutually supportive environment, you can explore and express together the feelings and memories that these exercises may evoke in you. However, if you cannot organize your time to share this process with a friend, you may follow the steps alone, simply reading aloud to yourself when it is time to read your list.

FINDING YOUR PERSONAL LIE

To find your Personal Lie, the most negative belief that you have about yourself, follow this simple exercise.

- Write the beginning of the sentence *"A negative thought I have about myself is . . ."* on a piece of paper. Finish this sentence with whatever comes to mind, regardless of how simplistic, negative, or irrelevant it may seem. This exercise should be done relatively quickly, without excessive reflection. Simply write what comes to mind, as it comes to mind.

- Repeat this process several times, always ending the sentence with something different.

- Be aware of how you feel as you compile the list. Pay attention to physical sensations, your breathing, and your emotional state. Notice how your inner state changes as you progress with the list.

- Once you have finished your list (when you cannot think of any other negative thoughts you have about yourself), read through the list several times out loud and mark the three or four sentences which disturb you the most. Signs of disturbance can include difficulties breathing, dry throat, cold hands, tension in the stomach, shoulders, and/or neck, and emotional reactions such as sadness and anger.

- Continue, by a process of elimination, to find the sentence that is the most disturbing for you. This sentence represents your Personal Lie, the most limiting belief you hold about yourself.

- Rewrite the sentence of your Personal Lie at the top of a fresh page and contemplate the meaning of the words you have written, allowing thoughts and memories associated with the sentence to come to your conscious awareness.

- Write down some of the ways that this negative belief has affected your behavior and self-expression during your life.

- Record the important experiences you have lived which are connected to your Personal Lie.

THE PERSONAL LIE AND POSTURE

- Repeat the words of your Personal Lie several times, both silently and aloud, slowly adopting the posture that corresponds to the feelings you discover as you repeat it.

- Allow your body to find the posture of your Personal Lie, exploring the relation between your respiration, posture, and inner emotional state.

- Note very carefully the way you feel in your body as a whole, as well as the sensations and impressions you discover in isolated parts of your body where you feel particularly tense.

- When you have found the posture that "feels right" to you, stay in it for several minutes, repeating the words of your Personal Lie from time to time.

- Continue to pay attention to your inner state, accepting as much as possible the different emotions and memories that may come and go.

- After some minutes, liberate yourself from your assumed posture, shaking off the accumulated tension in your body by walking around the room, stretching, and moving vigorously until you feel relaxed again.

Now that you have found your Personal Lie, you must pay attention to how it functions in your life. Become aware of the ways you express this belief and observe your behavior in various situations, noting the results this belief creates. In situations where you have a tendency to behave according to the belief of your Personal Lie, consciously choose to believe a different thought about yourself—a loving thought—and observe how the atmosphere changes when you modify your thoughts with awareness.

Some Examples of the Personal Lie

I'm not good enough.
I'm not acceptable.
I'm not lovable.
I don't deserve to be loved.
I'm not wanted.
I can't find my place in this world.
Nothing ever works for me.
Life is a struggle and I never succeed.
I can't express myself.
Nobody understands me.
It's not safe to trust.
I am betrayed by life.
I am insignificant.
I am not capable.
There is no hope for me.
I don't deserve to live.
I am stupid.
I cannot be myself.
I am weak and I have no defenses.
I struggle to live and to live is painful.
I deserve to be deprived and abandoned.

THE ETERNAL KEY

Affirmations are positive thoughts which are programmed into the subconscious mind by repetition and with awareness, to assist the process of personal transformation and self-realization. In intuition development, affirmations are used as a means to develop self-esteem, self-acceptance, and self-love. During personal meditation sessions, you use the affirmation of your Eternal Key to create a state of inner calm in which you can communicate with your intuitive self. Using the Eternal Key as an "antidote" to your Personal Lie, you will gradually transform your belief systems about yourself, at the same time transforming your physical posture, emotional habits, and sense of self-esteem.

Affirmations must be written in the first person *(I)*, in present tense *(I am, I have, I love, I feel)*, and should be relatively short and concise.

FINDING YOUR ETERNAL KEY

To create an Eternal Key for yourself, begin with your Personal Lie and rewrite it in a positive sense. For example, "I'm not acceptable" becomes "I'm acceptable." Now elaborate on this basic theme, until you find a sentence that really touches you and gives you a very positive feeling about yourself. For example, "I love and accept myself totally" or "I am acceptable and lovable exactly as I am."

Once you have chosen the Eternal Key that suits you, you must verify the effect it has on you. Repeat it aloud several times and pay attention to how you feel as you say it. What sensations do you have in your body? How do you feel emotionally? How does your breathing and posture change? Explore your posture while repeating the Eternal Key, until you find the postural attitude that corresponds to your inner attitude. Stay centered in this posture for several minutes, paying attention to how you feel in your body.

If you feel uplifted, inspired, and more joyful as you repeat the words of your Eternal Key, then you have chosen appropriately.

It is important that you utilize the Eternal Key consciously in your life, adopting the posture and respiration that corresponds to it and using it regularly in your meditation sessions. Apply your Eternal Key, as a preferred attitude, to various situations in your life, paying attention to how your changed attitude alters your perception of the experiences you live.

Some Examples of the Eternal Key

I am perfectly acceptable as I am.
I love and accept myself as I am.
I am loving, lovable, and loved.
I have my place and purpose in the world.
I know my life's purpose and I follow my path with joy.
I succeed naturally and gracefully in my life.
I express myself with ease and confidence.   ·
I understand and respect myself.
I trust myself.
I am free and I have everything I need.
Love is my birthright and I accept it now.
My presence in the world is appreciated and recognized.
I choose to be alive, here, in this body, now.
I am a source of divine light.
I shine.
The light of love flows in me and I share it in the world.
I am alive and I accept the energy of life within me.
I am a being of light, radiant.
I am sure of myself in all circumstances.
I exist and I am free to express myself as I am.

CHAPTER TEN

The Energetic Body

The concept of an energetic body or bodies, surrounding the physical body of all living beings, is a concept that has been debated and researched since antiquity. The existence of energetic emanations around plants, animals, and humans has been well explored and documented with the work of Kirlian photography, which clearly demonstrates fluctuations in intensity of energetic radiation depending on differing emotional states, as well as during periods of sickness and good health.

THE WORLD OF SUBTLE PERCEPTION

Metaphysical practitioners and students of esoteric practices who have personally explored the energetic body through meditation and "hands on" work agree unequivocally on the existence of an energy field surrounding and emanating from living beings. There are several differing schools of thought regarding the organization of these fields of energy, and regarding their ultimate function.

THE AURA

Depending on the tradition, philosophy, and personal experience of the individual, esoterics generally agree on the existence of between

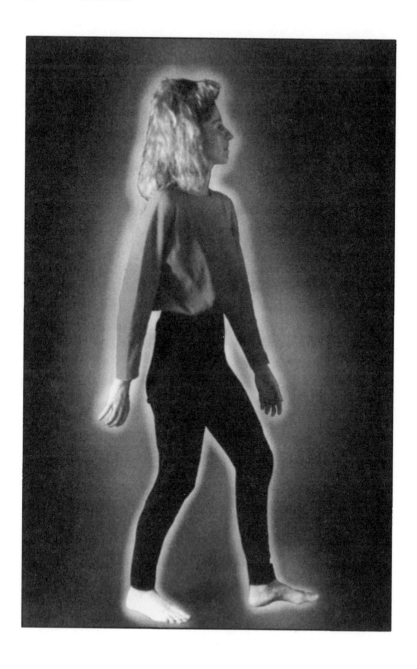

four and twelve different energetic fields surrounding the physical human body, each one corresponding to a level of consciousness of the individual. The energetic field, more commonly known as the aura, can be intuitively perceived and explored using touch, feeling, and vision to gain information and insights into the current state of oneself or of another. From an intuitive perspective, the aura can be likened to an intricately woven tapestry of light and color enveloping its owner in an ever changing landscape of sensation, mood, and movement. The aura is, by its nature, a flowing energetic field of colors, feelings, and thoughts, existing in a form too subtle to be seen by the normal human eye, yet perceptible through intuitive inner vision. All that exists in the aura exists as a reflection or an overflow, of what exists in our inner world of being. The aura is an external manifestation of our inner state, reflecting in a more subtle form the physical, emotional, mental, and spiritual levels of being. The emanations of the aura are the result of the function of energy fields existing in the interior of the physical body. We find the energy axis located along the vertebral column, extending toward the earth from the base of the spine, and toward heaven from the crown of the head. The energetic body is sustained by this vertical axis, which absorbs subtle light nourishment from the air above and the earth below the physical body. Aligned within the axis and following the vertebral column are several individual spheres of energetic matter. These energy fields, or centers, are known as chakras and, together with the axis and the aura, they combine to create the energetic body of living beings.

THE CHAKRAS

A chakra is a concentration of energy within a living being, situated in a strategic part of the body. Intuitively perceived, this energy often resembles a sphere, a funnel, or a spinning cone in shape. The word *chakra* has its roots in the Sanskrit language and translates as "wheel that turns." There are seven major chakras in the human body and

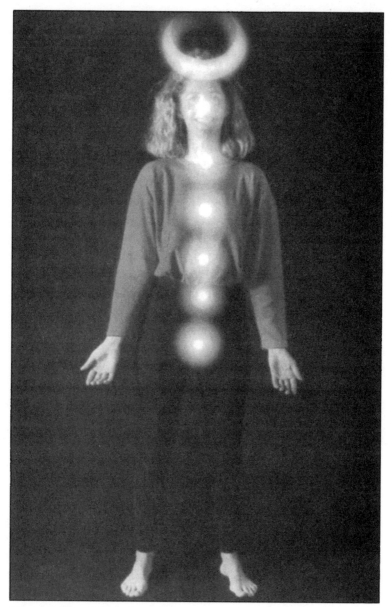

Figure 3. The chakras: front view.

numerous minor ones, with four of particular importance located in the palms of the hands and on the feet. The seven major chakras are aligned along the axis of the body, beginning at the base of the pelvis and ascending to the crown of the head.

From a metaphysical point of view, the chakras are considered as energy centers of the subtle body that act directly on the physical body through their interrelation with the glandular (hormonal) system. The chakra centers receive, store, and radiate life-force energy, which is absorbed through the respiratory system, the skin, and the eyes (as light) throughout the lifetime of an individual.

During the interaction between a person and the external world, a constant exchange of subtle energies occurs that directly affects the vitality level of the individual, as well as the well-being of the energetic body.

When we interrelate with the external world, the energy, or light, generated by the interrelationship is received into our bodies through one or several of the chakras. The generated energy is stored in the subtle body as an experience and in the physical body as a body memory. The memories held in both the subtle and physical bodies have an emotional, as well as a mental, component. The experience lived, our subjective analysis of it, and our emotional and physical responses to it are all registered and stored. Every time we interact with the external world, with nature, and with other living beings, we receive energy during the encounters. Every time we express ourselves, we radiate life-force energy through the chakras, giving energy to the external world. This constant process of give and take, present in the interrelationships between all living beings, creates movement, circulation, and change, qualities essential to the well-being of both the physical and energetic bodies.

The chakras contain memories of all the experiences we have lived through time, both in this life and in other lives. The most ancient memories are stored deep in the core of the chakras, while more recent memories are held closer to their surface, corresponding

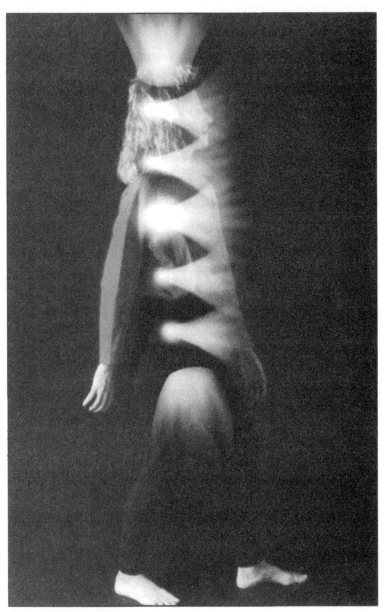

Figure 4. The chakras: side view.

also to the surface of the physical body. Every time we enter into contact with another, physically, emotionally, mentally, or psychically, we enter into contact with the totality of their experience, with the totality of their memories. Of course, for most people, this process occurs and is experienced at an unconscious level. Nevertheless, every single time we enter into an exchange with someone, this "memory bank" of experience is stimulated. The quality of exchange we experience with another is always determined, to a greater or lesser degree, by the ensemble of memories triggered during the exchange. This "remembering" can occur at a conscious, subconscious, or unconscious level in both of the parties involved in the exchange.

Every exchange, however superficial or profound, is remembered by the body/being on a vibrational (sensational), emotional, intellectual, and spiritual (soul) level.

The role and functioning of the chakras is of fundamental importance in the healing and transformational journey of the human being. It is into this "memory pool" of the four levels of being that we dip to access past traumas, to locate, define, and address unfinished business, and to find and understand energy blockages and physical illnesses in the body. Through the stored information in the chakras, we can locate and reanimate forgotten and neglected inner resources, qualities that assist us to strengthen, realign, and heal our physical, as well as our subtle, body. It is through the structure and function of the chakra system that we can retrace the paths of our personal and symbolic story, finding our way through the recent and more ancient past, until we arrive at the deepest memory of the chakras, the memory of our essential self. Here we are always strong, pure, and unmarked by the hazards of the experiences of life. In this deep part of the chakras, we are connected to our vertical axis and the axis is connected to the stabilizing influence of Earth energy and the uplifting, illuminating influence of heavenly (universal) energy. The energies of Earth and universe constantly nourish, replenish, and refortify the chakra system, cleansing and purifying the energetic body. The connection and interrelation between the chakras, the axis, the Earth, and the universe, are essential to the health, well-being, and evolutionary possibilities of the human being.

Each of the seven major chakras of the human being are related to a sphere of activity in human life, as well as to a level of consciousness related to the inner world of the individual. A chakra can be functional without the conscious awareness of its "owner," in the same way that our organs and other bodily systems function without our conscious direction. Because the chakras belong to the energetic body and are therefore very subtle in their nature, they are particularly susceptible to conscious awareness and direction. Once we become aware of the existence of the chakra system, our very awareness creates movement, change, and evolution in this part of ourselves. It is possible, through acting on the chakras with thought and imagination, to act, eventually, on the physical body itself, creating change, transformation, and healing. Before acting on the chakras however, it is essential to understand what they are, where they are, and how they influence our lives.

First Chakra

The first chakra is located at the base of the spine in the genital region. It governs general physical constitution, circulation in the lower body, sexuality, and all basic survival issues. Life-force energy that flows at this level of the body/being is concerned with essential survival needs of the human being—the necessity for food and shelter which then becomes a question of work and money. In this chakra, your energy is used to take care of the fundamental details of daily life. The first chakra also governs your essential sexual energy, the sexual organs, the ovaries and prostate glands, the organs of elimination (colon, bladder, and skin), and the circulation of energy in the pelvis, legs, and feet. The state of the first chakra (open, flowing, irregular, blocked, closed, etc.) describes your fundamental existence and determines the way you go forward in your life—the way you advance physically and temperamentally through life. If this chakra is open and the energy circulates well, your body will be constitutionally strong and generally healthy, your sexual energy will be lively and consistent, and you will advance progressively in your life at the rhythm that is correct for you, experiencing improvements in your standard of living as you find your way to manage and master survival needs.

Through the first chakra, you create a connection to the Earth and take care of earthly concerns (material details). The more this chakra is open and flowing, the more grounded you will be. The more you are grounded, the more you will be a master of the material details of life and the more pleasure you will experience in being alive, present, in a body, on this Earth.

If, as a soul, you are troubled by the fact that you are in a body, that is, you are not certain that you really want to be here, this inner dilemma will be evident as problems and energetic blockages in the pelvis, legs, and feet. If, for example, you made the decision as a soul to incarnate in a body, but discovered that life on Earth is more difficult, bothersome, and impossible to understand than you remembered, a situation is created where energetically you try (as a soul) to leave your body to "go home." You pull away from the Earth and you pull away from your physical body, against the natural current of life-force energy, which flows into you from heaven toward the Earth, propelling you gently forward along your evolutionary path.

The result is that you go against the natural flow. You close yourself to the energies flowing naturally in your body and all around you, and you experience tension and physical pain. Over time, a closed and blocked first chakra causes circulation problems in the feet and legs, as well as problems in the ankles and knees, and in the articulations of the toes. Lack of sexual energy, sexual impulse and interest, frigidity, impotence, bladder infections, and constipation are all signs of first-chakra malfunction. Other indications of problems at this level include lack of vitality, a waning enthusiasm for life, and the lack of a sense of direction in life.

If you are tense and cannot let go physically, or, conversely, if you are too slack (without tone and tension), you may have a first-chakra problem that is often related to the question of your basic desire to be alive. If you have constant problems about money, about finding a profession that is really suitable for you, about finding a home that pleases you, you are being shown that your deeper problem is related to the question of existing at all. You have, perhaps, a deep ambivalence about life itself and, therefore, you hesitate to commit yourself deeply and fully to life. In fact, you are not really here yet, even though you are alive and living.

If you want to be well in your body, in a home you enjoy, and with work that satisfies you, you must commit yourself more deeply to life. You must be willing to open to the flow of life, to engage with life, to go with life. It is important to enter more fully into contact with your physical body and to be willing to explore and transform the fears that you have about being alive, about letting go into the flow of life.

Once your first chakra is open and flowing and you are well grounded and present in life, you will become more and more aware of the energy that flows into you and through you—energy from the universe, the earth, and from others. You will feel yourself strong, lively, and energetic, willing to go forward, willing to advance.

The key words for the first chakra are "*I exist.*"

Second Chakra

The second chakra is located in the pelvic area, just below the navel, in the mound of the belly. This energy center relates to your emotional experience—the ebb and flow of emotional states within you, as well as your emotional relationships with others. Your sexuality is expressed through this chakra in the quality of sensual response, rather than the first-chakra physical need and biological urge to procreate. Through your second chakra, you feel the desire to share something of yourself with another, to reveal your vulnerability, and to share your sensitivity and passion through the exchange of a personal relationship.

The second chakra also describes the way you nourish yourself emotionally. In the first chakra, you nourish yourself to stay alive, while at the level of the second chakra, you nourish yourself to feel loved. In this center of consciousness, you discover your needs, your emotional desires and your urge to belong, to have a place. The way that you approach others and enter into intimate relationships with them, the fluidity with which you adapt yourself to changes in your life, and the rhythm of your inner emotional movement are all behaviors related to the functioning of this chakra. The emotional inner world being changeable and fluid in its nature, movement and spontaneity are very important qualities associated with the well-being of this aspect of yourself.

Corresponding equally to the qualities of receptivity and femininity, the second chakra is related to the mother—how you were mothered and, as a result, how you mother yourself and others. Did you get touched enough, cradled enough, cuddled enough, fed enough when you were a child? Was the quality of contact that you received enough to satisfy your needs? Was your mother in her heart with you? Was she really there, present and attentive to your needs? Or did you, in fact, feel smothered by her? Never free from her presence? Now, in your adult life, do you seek touch and find contact easy, or is contact something you tend to avoid? The relationship your mother had with her body often influences the relationship you have with your own body.

The small intestine, the organ responsible for the assimilation of nourishment, is influenced by the function of the second chakra, as are the uterus (in women), the kidneys, and the adrenal glands. If you have problems in this zone of the body and in these organs, they are often related to the mother and, in particular, to the way you feel you were mothered. Either through lack or through smothering, the result is an imbalance in your emotional function and the way you manage your intimate relationships. If your mother neglected you, you may crave attention, yet never feel satisfied with the quality of attention you receive. To fulfill your need for physical contact and reassurance, you may play the seduction game to excess, seeking endlessly after the quality of maternal nourishment you missed and finding some comfort through the sensual and sexual contact of intimate adult relationships. Or, if your mother smothered you with attention, you may have adopted a cold, self-protective manner to keep others at a distance, unconsciously proving to yourself and to your mother that you are free of her.

The emotional needs of the second chakra are strongly related to the unconscious needs of the child within, especially the unfulfilled needs of childhood: the need for security, attention, and tenderness; the need for exploration, adventure, and freedom; the need to feel special, unique, and appreciated. Given the demands of children and the difficulties experienced by most parents in responding adequately to these demands, it is a rare child who arrives at adulthood feeling they were understood, unconditionally accepted, emotionally fulfilled, and adequately nourished by their parents.

Problems of the small intestine indicate unresolved issues concerning nourishment. You may need to learn how to nourish your body with a balanced diet, taking the time to learn to combine and prepare foods in a manner that corresponds to your particular and unique dietary needs. Physical nourishment is essential to well-being and regular, moderate eating habits can often rectify some of the chronic assimilation problems of the small intestines. The "modern" diseases of anorexia and bulimia experienced by adolescent girls and women have their roots in questions and issues relating to the mother, nourishment, and the female image—all issues governed by the second chakra. The uterus and ovaries, so essential to the creative nourishing process of procreation, can only function well if a woman nourishes herself in a balanced fashion. The kidneys, eliminators of body toxins, require regular liquid nourishment to accomplish their task adequately.

Even though attention to diet is an essential and important step in healing problems of the second chakra, a more fundamental need is, in fact, that of emotional nourishment. Malfunctioning of the second chakra indicates the need for maturation of the emotional self. You must become adult, your own mother, so you can let go of your emotional dependence on others and establish mature relationships based on the mutual desire to share and exchange.

When your second chakra is open and functioning in a balanced rhythm, you can feel the richness, the diversity of your emotional self, and sense instinctively the rhythms of distance and intimacy in your personal relationships. You can maintain the feeling of your relationship to the other—your sense of place—and yet remain aware of your rhythms, which are unique to you. With the healthy functioning of your second chakra, you can trust in the spontaneous expression of your emotions, which add movement, depth, and meaning to your daily life.

The key words that describe the functioning of the second chakra are "*I feel.*"

Third Chakra

The third chakra is located in the solar plexus, above the navel, in the region of the diaphragm. This chakra, like the second, is emotional in nature, but its function describes the way you direct your emotional needs and desires into the world, rather than the way you feel yourself in relation to the world.

The third chakra is your power center, describing your will-power and stamina. Its function determines the way you direct your life. Through your third chakra, you transform your ideas into reality—you build your world according to your emotional needs and desires, and according to your belief systems. Through the experience of your second chakra you feel your place in relation to your mother, the family, and the world. Through the dynamics of the third chakra, you create your place in the world—you take your place.

This chakra represents the masculine energy in you—your expressive, male aspect and, therefore, also the father. How were you fathered? How were you disciplined when you were young? What was your relationship to authority? How was your life organized in the family? Were you taught the value of order, of structure? Were you guided by your parents to bring a concept through to reality with the help of the structure of discipline and organization? Were you, in fact, controlled to the point where you felt powerless, unimportant? Or were you fathered in such a way that you felt incapable of succeeding yourself? How do you discipline yourself now?

To better understand the current state of your third chakra, it may be fruitful to pay attention to how you structure your life, to the way you organize yourself. Do you exert a lot of self-control? Are you a leader? Do you take charge of situations? Or are you a follower? This center of energy determines whether you take the position of victim or creator in your life, whether your life is something that happens to you, or whether you take charge and steer your life according to your preferences. Are you someone who often feels manipulated, used? A doormat? Or do you stand up for yourself? Do you, in fact, have a tendency to stand on others?

The organs which come under the rulership of the third chakra are the liver, gall bladder, stomach, pancreas, and spleen. If the circulation of your energy is blocked in the third chakra, you will probably have problems in the function of one or several of these organs. The diaphragm, a large muscle situated in the solar plexus, is directly related to the third chakra and the respiratory process. Breathing problems are, therefore, often associated with blockage of energy flow in the third chakra.

If you are someone who never gets angry or who does not express anger, you most certainly have a blockage in this region! If you are someone who is chronically angry, you have a third-chakra problem. If you never feel afraid, if you live in a state of constant fear, if you never stop doing, if you never start doing, if you experience extremes like this in your emotional makeup, you are experiencing an imbalance in the energetic function of your third chakra.

Both the second and third chakras describe your inner emotional life and the fashion in which you express yourself emotionally with others, in intimacy and in a more general way, in relation to the world at large. To become really mature you must resolve your relationships to both the mother and the father. To become emotionally mature, you must understand the ways you were conditioned by the behavioral tendencies of your parents and free yourself from this programming.

When your third chakra functions in a healthy and balanced way, you discover your capacity to bring dreams to life through discipline, organization, and determination. You create a goal and, with time, realize it. Through the function of your third chakra, you feel yourself as a powerful, self-determined being, capable of making a unique and creative contribution in your chosen sphere of life. By nature, you are firm in your ideas, but you can also be flexible and accommodating when you work with others to bring an idea into realization.

The key words to describe the third chakra are "*I create.*"

• • •

The life issues governed by the first three chakras take a tremendous amount of time in most peoples lives. The necessity for food, shelter, work, and personal relationships create the fundamental occupations of life and can also create great hardships. When you function principally through these three chakras, your experience is very subjective—you are inside your experience of life, living what comes toward you and reacting to it.

Fourth Chakra

The fourth chakra, the chakra of the heart, plays an enormous role in recognizing and understanding your potential as an individual. This chakra acts as a point of integration for the other chakras, as it contains elements of the four levels of your experience: physical, emotional, mental, and spiritual. Through the fourth chakra, located in the center of the chest, you integrate the experiences of life and develop the qualities of wisdom and compassion. With this level of consciousness, you become a true friend to others, not because you need something, but simply for the joy of it, for the pleasure of the exchange. The generosity of your spirit lives in the heart chakra— the desire to give to others, to share your experiences, to find and express that which you have in common with your fellow humans.

The heart chakra is the home of the soul. When you are incarnated in a body, your soul rests in the depths of your fourth chakra, living, witnessing, absorbing, and integrating the experiences you gather on your path through life. In the heart chakra, you develop the qualities of unconditional love and detachment in relation to the exterior world. You know you are in the world, but not of it. When your awareness is focused in this chakra, you are with yourself and you can be with others, without losing yourself. In the second chakra, when you are with another, you tend to merge, dissolve, and lose yourself in the flow of the exchange. In the fourth-chakra exchange, you are present, yourself, whole and compassionate, engaged in the exchange, yet with a certain detachment from personal need.

The organs of the body which are governed by the fourth chakra are the heart, the lungs, and the thymus gland. Problems at this level include high blood pressure, low blood pressure, heart-valve problems, blood and circulatory difficulties, respiratory infections, hyperventilation, hypoventilation, mid-back pain, and pneumonia. All of these problems are indications of a deeper conflict concerning the absorption and integration of life experience.

Through your lungs, you breathe in air and absorb the life force flowing all around you. From the air, oxygen is integrated into your body by your lungs and absorbed into your blood, where it is pumped by the heart throughout the entire body. Once the oxygenated blood is distributed and your body nourished (that is, the oxygenated blood is digested), that which is no longer useful is eliminated and sent through your heart to the lungs, where it is expelled as carbon dioxide. These two organs regulate the flow of essential life-force energy into and out of your body, while the fourth chakra regulates the flow of essential life experience into and out of your body.

Sadness and joy are the two emotional extremes expressed through the function of the heart chakra. If you experience much sadness in your life, it can be helpful to understand this sadness as the expression of one aspect of your soul. What makes you deeply sad? What are you missing? Are you nostalgic for your connection to the Source, to God? Are you sad that you cannot find your real people, your real tribe, your true healing family? Do you feel lost? Perhaps you feel you have lost your way, your friends, your feeling of being connected, your sense of fellowship? In the sadness of the heart chakra, there is often a longing, a nostalgia for something forgotten, something lost.

Even when life is rich and you feel fortunate, privileged compared to others around you, the sense of a lack, or a loss, is still there. This lack has nothing to do with the material organization of your life, but is the grief-call of your soul longing for a quality of life experience you lack. It is the call of your soul, longing for you to be inside yourself, to be with yourself, to listen to the needs of your heart, and to cultivate a quality of life that is rich, deep, and authentic.

If you are well integrated in your heart chakra, you will be joyful and playful, with a lively sense of humor. You will appreciate the ironies of life, accepting the paradoxes and dualities by which you are surrounded with a knowing wisdom. Even though you will be sincere and kind to others, you will retain your authenticity and honesty, always staying faithful to your truth, which is as unique as you are.

Faced with the problems of others and the problems of a lost and troubled world, you will maintain a compassionate yet detached position, knowing that problems are a necessary and unavoidable part of life, essential for evolution. Integrated in your heart chakra, you experience a lightness of heart, a lightness of being, which is not at all superficial, but is, rather, a lightness that comes from knowing yourself and respecting your limits in the face of the needs and problems of others.

If you have lost your sense of humor, your ability to laugh at yourself and the ironies of life, you are suffering from a malady of the heart, a serious illness. If you have this problem, there is a reason for it. There is something important missing from your life. There is a quality you need, which you are not receiving. Perhaps it is a quality of friendship, support, or fellowship, or the feeling of being understood. Maybe you need to let go of the past to be more available in your present life. Very often, unfinished business from the past, with family, coworkers, and friends, creates an emotional weight in the heart that cannot be shaken until it is addressed and resolved.

The key words for the fourth chakra are "*I love.*"

Fifth Chakra

The fifth chakra is found in the throat and represents the functioning of the conscious rational mind, with its ability to analyze, compartmentalize, and discriminate. This chakra governs communication—speaking, listening, and understanding spoken words, and then organizing these words into a frame of reference suited to your personal belief systems.

If you experience muscular problems in your neck, in the cervical vertebrae, have chronic throat infections, hearing difficulties, and/or mouth and teeth problems, there is a direct relationship to the fifth-chakra function of the rational mind and communication. Because this chakra governs the expression of your ideas, it also represents the way you interpret the ideas and verbal expressions of others. Do you listen when others speak to you? Do you think others listen to you? Are your ideas important and valuable? Do you express yourself clearly? Can you express your needs in such a way that you feel understood? Do you hear what people say to you? Are you able to organize your thoughts in such a way that you can follow your own ideas logically? Can you paraphrase an idea or a problem?

If you believe you are unimportant and have low self-esteem, it can be difficult to express yourself with words. As you begin to speak, others turn and look at you, waiting for you to continue your sentence, your story. If you are not sure of yourself, it is easy to wind down a sentence before it is finished, leaving yourself and everyone else "hanging in midair," wondering what the point or purpose of your communication was. The result is that you have not expressed yourself and the others have not understood you.

Many fifth-chakra problems are related to the self-image instilled in you as a child. If your parents did not take enough time to help you find the words with which to express yourself, you can think unconsciously that others have no time for you or that your ideas have no value. If, as a child, you were shy and found it difficult to express yourself spontaneously, others more sophisticated than you may have judged you as slow or stupid and you may have kept this judgment as an idea about yourself, even though it is not appropriate.

The solution to almost all problems of the fifth chakra can be found in communication and expression. What do you need to say? To whom? With what tone of voice? In which emotional state? What words do you need to use so that your expression can be heard and understood by others? How can you express yourself honestly, authentically?

With the fifth chakra and communication, it is essential to speak for yourself, from your own experience, never assuming you know the reality of someone else. If you wish to be heard by others, it is essential that you do not attack them with judgments and accusations. If you are angry because you have felt hurt by the actions of others, it is important that you express your anger. However, if you hold the others responsible for your hurt and anger, you can be sure they will not be available to listen to your tirade against them. It is imperative to learn a few simple rules for effective communication so that you can find the way to speak clearly, simply, and with conviction about your ideas, feelings and experiences.

When your fifth chakra is functioning in a balanced and integrated fashion, you express yourself with ease in the majority of situations, whether in a large group or in intimacy with another. You speak clearly and fluently, finding the appropriate nuance to express the idea you wish to share. In the same way, you are able to listen to and hear others when they speak to you, allowing them to finish their sentences before you respond. You are open-minded to the ideas of others, while staying faithful to your own experience of life. Mentally organized and able to handle efficiently the details of your daily life, you are able to manage your time effectively, arriving on time for your appointments. You are able to plan in advance and carry your plan through to completion, paying attention to details as you go, so that the end result is what you have worked for. With your fifth chakra open, flowing, and balanced, you are able to communicate your needs to people, who are available to listen to you. Your experience of communication supports you in your belief that you can be honest and authentic without being judgmental and that the words you speak have a true value.

The key words for the fifth chakra are "*I communicate.*"

Sixth Chakra

The sixth chakra is found in the center of the head behind the fore-head and governs the function of the subconscious and the unconscious mind. This is where your imagination functions—where you see things, internally and externally. The sixth chakra determines your ability to see with perspective, with distance. This is the home of your clairvoyance (clear seeing). With this chakra, you perceive and understand the patterns of events and the cycles of life that occur all around you. With the perspective of your sixth-chakra vision, you understand the behavior of others, seeing their psychological patterns and behavioral habits in relation to yourself, to themselves, and to others. With your second chakra, you experience the behavior of the other; with your fourth chakra, you accept it as it is; with your sixth chakra, you see it clearly and understand it. You perceive how it fits into a bigger picture, so you have distance and perspective.

In the sixth chakra, you find all the functions of the brain and mind. It is in this chakra that your belief systems about life are stored and expressed as the creative functioning of your mind. Belief systems created through the experience of life are often deeply buried in the unconscious mind and function as an immediate reflex reaction in response to life situations. Through the natural interrelation between your sixth and fifth chakras, your belief systems are expressed through the symbology of your dreams, the action of your imagination, and the communication of your ideas.

In your sixth chakra, you hold the idea you have of yourself—of how you look (whether you are beautiful, ugly, ordinary, fat, thin) and of how you characteristically behave in given situations (clumsily, gracefully, stupidly, intelligently). This idea, this self-image, is based on past personal experience and specific conditioning and programming you received as an infant. According to the idea you have of yourself (of your strengths and weaknesses), you see yourself as having one place or another in the world. With the creative power of your imagination always supporting your personal belief systems, you create for yourself the place you believe you deserve. It can be said of the sixth chakra that, with this aspect of yourself, you create yourself, your world, and your place in it. If you change your creative idea of yourself, you will change your external reality naturally, because of the creative power of your imagination.

How do you imagine yourself? What are your positive and negative qualities? When you look in a mirror, real or imaginary, what do you see? Your sixth chakra is a mirror, reflecting you back to yourself, continuously showing you the beliefs you have about yourself, about others, about life. Are you aware of the power of your imagination? Can you direct your imagination to create a vision internally and hold that vision until it is manifest in the external world around you? Can you look around you and perceive the patterns, the cycles of behavior unfolding—the cycles of nature, of Earth, of people, of yourself?

Physical problems related to the sixth chakra include headaches, migraines, neck pain, and eyesight disorders. What is it that you do not want to see? What is too difficult to see? To what are you too close? From what do you take so much distance that you can no longer see clearly? What creates pain in your head? What thoughts and beliefs make you sick of yourself? What do you see in yourself, about yourself, that you cannot, will not, accept? In others? In the world?

When the sixth chakra is blocked, related reactions are often "I don't want to see!" Or, "I don't want to take responsibility." If you have difficulties perceiving, understanding, and accepting responsibility for your ideas, dreams, and actions, this is often a manifestation of a sixth chakra blockage.

When the sixth chakra is functioning well, you will have a vivid imagination, with clear, detailed images that come and go easily on the screen of your creative mind. You will experience life as an ongoing series of interconnected events, each with a significance and a symbolic meaning evident to you. In the rhythm and flow of the ever changing cycles unfolding within you and around you, you will see your place, your role, and your own significance in relation to others. Life appears as a rich tapestry of sensation, feelings, and images, and you, the weaver, work the tapestry in relation to the experiences you live. With the richness of your flowing imagination, you know you are the dreamer and the dream. You understand that truth is relative, that everyone is right from their own point of view. You free yourself from the limitations of your programmed belief systems and explore the unlimited possibilities of your creative imagination.

The key words for the sixth chakra are "*I see.*"

Seventh Chakra

The seventh chakra, at the crown of the head, reaches out toward the universe. It it the chakra of your spiritual self, which governs not only your spiritual beliefs and practices, but also the religious conditioning you received as a child. The crown chakra describes your sense of connection to the universe, to the Source, to God, in whatever form you believe Him to exist. In this chakra, you experience your sense of purpose—the reason why, as a spiritual being, you have incarnated into a body, the reason why you have come to Earth.

If you have blockages at the level of your seventh chakra, they may manifest physically as headaches and tension in the region of the head, neck, and shoulders. More often, seventh-chakra problems manifest as a sense of confusion and lack of a sense of purpose.

Energy-circulation problems here can be experienced as a feeling of being cut off from life and others, or through the lack of belief in an infinite intelligence, in God, in light.

Do you feel that your life has a purpose? Do you believe that the universe is intelligent? That humanity is evolving? Do you feel that you are a light being, living in a physical body, gathering experience on your evolutionary journey back home to the Source? Do you go forward in trust, with faith that you will find your way? Do you feel guided?

When your seventh chakra is open and functioning, you feel yourself on your path, going somewhere with a sense of purpose. You have faith, but this faith is not a blind faith—it is a faith full of questions. You are curious—curious to search, to research, and to discover what life is. You wish to find and explore mysteries, to experience nature and the vast universe. With your connection to the Source, to the light, you experience your uniqueness, your deepness, your vastness, and your nothingness. Through your seventh-chakra aspect, you can experience the fullness of the emptiness within you—to understand the significance of your place and your purpose against the vast backdrop of the ever present universe. You will be able to live your purpose fully, knowing that your life is but a cycle of experience and that one day, you will die to this life and go on to the Source from which you came, from which all existence comes and to which it goes. This you will know with acceptance in your heart, for you understand that we are all but visitors to this Earth and that, to live, we must die to a greater life we leave behind us—a greater life to which we eventually return.

The key words for the seventh chakra are "*I know.*"

• • •

It can be helpful, in understanding the chakras, to regard them as either expressive or receptive. The first, third, and fifth chakras are expressive, active, masculine, and yang in character, while the second, fourth, and sixth chakras are receptive, passive, feminine, and yin in character.

With the energy of the expressive chakras you act—you move, you create, you communicate, you reach out. If the movement of your energy is blocked in these chakras, you will have a problem "doing." The remedy for this problem is action and expression. You need to move physically—walk, run, dance, shake. You need to express your innate power by changing the organization of the physical world around you. Work in the garden, change the placement of furniture in your home, build something, destroy and throw away something else.

You need to communicate, to express who you are with words— you may speak, yell, scream, and write letters to important people in your life. Blockages of energy circulation in the expressive chakras are related to problems of repression—of holding back. What are you holding back? Why are you holding back? Why are you afraid of stepping out, of going forward? If you express yourself, what is the worst thing you imagine can happen to you? If you dare to be yourself and take your place in the world, what is the best thing you imagine can happen to you?

With the energy of the receptive chakras, you receive, feel, perceive, understand, and integrate. The natural movement of these chakras is an inward flow, taking you toward your deepness, to your inner perceptivity and awareness. If you experience difficulties with your sensitive, receptive, feminine aspects and these chakras are blocked, you may need to go within yourself more deeply. You need to feel more, to listen more, and to be more available, above all, to yourself. Very often, when the receptive chakras have functional difficulties, it is because you have a habit of living your life at a superficial level—you look outside yourself to find your sense of self, rather than seeking your truth in your inner deepness.

Energy blockages in the receptive chakras reveal your fear of discovering the truth of who you are. Energy blockages in the expressive chakras reveal your fear of expressing the truth of who you are.

The seventh chakra is both receptive and expressive. In receptive contemplation you understand the purpose of your life, and in expressive action, you realize this purpose.

A healthy body is a body where energy circulates in balance and harmony. Life-force energy, by its nature, is always in movement. When you repress the life-force energy within you—when you suppress your ideas, your feelings, and the natural urges of your physical body to move, the energy flowing through your chakras becomes blocked and stagnant. When this energy stops flowing correctly, you can experience physical discomfort, pain, illness, and disharmony in the part of your body affected by the blockage.

If your energy flow has stopped circulating in a region of your body and you wish to reanimate this part of yourself, it is very often difficult and painful at the beginning. It is as though something in you has died and you must bring it back to life. After an initial period of discomfort, you succeed in reawakening the chakra/body region and, from this point on, healthy circulation returns and you experience a decrease in pain and an increase in ease.

In the meditation of circulating Earth and universal energy into your heart chakra and throughout your subtle body, you are, in effect, calling your body back to life. This meditation is an affirmation of your desire and your willingness to be alive, vital, and complete. You choose consciously to call life-force energy into you, to nourish you and strengthen your subtle and physical bodies. Life-force energy naturally flows in through the first and seventh chakras if it can (if the energy pathways are not blocked). The pathways for this circulation of energy are already installed in you, whether you are consciously aware of them or not. When you become consciously aware of their existence, you can assist the pathways to function more efficiently. You can consciously direct Earth and universal energy to go where you want or need it to go.

If you have problems in a particular chakra, for example in the first chakra, you can heal these problems consciously. You can become more active physically, by walking, running, exercising. You can focus on grounding yourself by consciously developing suppleness in your knees, by connecting yourself more often with the earth, by bringing awareness to your pelvic area and breathing deeply and fully into this area of your body. In relation to the first chakra, you can engage in a work of personal therapy on the subject of your sexuality, to bring your life-force vitality back into this region of your body. If you have problems at the third chakra level about power, you can work consciously on this aspect of yourself. In your personal meditation you can bring Earth/universe energy into this chakra, cleansing, revitalizing, and strengthening this area of your body. Understanding the importance of self-expression in relation to your personal evolution, you can practice taking risks, you can allow yourself to become angry, to express your fear.

There are many ways you can help yourself to heal yourself, especially once you know and understand where your energy is blocked in your body and to what aspect of yourself that blockage corresponds.

The map of the chakras is a very useful system for clarifying the human subtle body system and its relationship to the physical body. However, you must always remember it is simply a map of the body, of the being—it is not The Being. Because you are unique, your problems are unique. Through the practice of the Chakra Meditation, you can understand more deeply your uniqueness, the uniqueness of your problems, and the uniqueness of the healing path you must take to restore yourself to a full and balanced state of well-being.

3

DEVELOPING YOUR
INTUITION:
CREATING THE
INNER STRUCTURE

CHAPTER ELEVEN

The Ritual of Inner Preparation

We begin to develop our intuition by adopting a regular meditation practice during which we create the appropriate inner structure and atmosphere through which our intuition can function.

There are several progressive steps to follow during the meditation of inner preparation. These steps should be followed systematically until their practice becomes second nature during meditation sessions. In the beginning, it is advisable to practice them one by one. After having experienced each meditation individually, you can practice them all together during one sitting.

The steps of the Ritual of Inner Preparation are as follows:

- Breathing
- Resource Natural Setting and Inner Temple
- Axis/Grounding
- Flowing Light
- Circle of Protection
- Anchoring Intuitive Mode

To benefit fully from the preparatory steps which create the inner structure essential to the functioning of the intuition, you must practice regularly. Program into your daily schedule a period of time between twenty minutes and one hour, during which you systemat-

Meditation posture: seated on the floor (figure 5, front view, and figure 6, side view).

Meditation posture: seated in a chair (figure 7, front view, and figure 8, side view).

ically practice the meditation and visualization techniques presented in this chapter.

For many people, the best time of the day for meditation is the morning, before daily activities begin. Another possible moment is at the end of the day, before retiring. When beginning, give yourself twenty minutes and slowly increase the amount of time you spend in each session. The more time you spend practicing, the more your intuition will develop and the more you will benefit from the engagement of your time. If you have a tendency to worry about time, you can use an alarm clock for your sessions. Set the alarm for the desired amount of time and begin your session. Give yourself two or three minutes after finishing your meditation to readapt yourself to the external world before resuming your other activities.

It is important that you create a quiet place you can go to for your sessions, and that you feel comfortable in this space. You can meditate in bed, in a comfortable chair, or sitting on the floor on a cushion with your legs crossed. It is essential for practice that your back be straight and your shoulders relaxed. You should wear unrestrictive clothing that allows you to breathe in both belly and chest. If you wear glasses, remove them before beginning the session. It is also advisable to remove your shoes.

To assist the flow of each meditation, it can be useful to have the guidance of a voice leading you through the several steps of inner preparation. Using the guidelines of the text, you may create a meditation by recording your own voice onto a cassette. You can also read and memorize the text of the written meditations and remind yourself of the steps as you practice. Alternatively, you can work with a friend, leading each other through the exercises and, afterward, sharing the feelings, images and messages you have received during the session.

BREATHING, RELAXATION, AWARENESS

The breath is our connection to life, the means through which our survival is assured. Essential to life, and essential also to our well-being, the breath is a wonderfully simple and effective tool for altering inner states of awareness. Too often taken for granted or completely ignored, the breath has become a forgotten wonder, a function that occurs, luckily, without need of our conscious intervention. Bringing our awareness to the breath reveals the importance and essential power present in this bodily function. The breath is a direct reflection of our state of being, of the way we live within our bodies. It is through the breathing process that we express our willingness to receive life-force energy and light into our bodies, into our lives. In the constant rhythmic movement of inspiration/expiration, we participate in the very movement of life all around us. At birth, we begin with the breath and it is through the breath that we take the first steps of coming back to ourselves in the practice of meditation.

Breathing Meditation

- Begin by breathing deeply and fully, taking several deep breaths, connecting the inhale to the exhale, on every out breath feel your body relaxing, letting go . . . allowing tension to leave you.

- As you breathe, become aware of the areas of your body where you feel tense and breathe into those parts, imagining the in breath is loosening the tension and the out breath is carrying it out of you, letting go of stress and tension on every out breath, breathing it out, letting it go, creating space inside you to relax, creating space inside you to receive the next in breath, relaxing more and more with each cycle of your breathing . . .

- Be aware of your body, of sensations existing in your body and be aware of your feelings, of the mood you are in, the emotional state you feel as you breathe, as you relax, as you let go . . .

- Notice your mind, your thoughts as they come and go, simply observing, being aware . . . letting thoughts and feelings flow and as they flow, letting go with every out breath, relaxing and releasing tension, relaxing . . . allowing the tensions to melt, to dissolve and disappear with the slow, steady rhythm of your breath coming and going . . . relaxing and aware . . . calm.

RESOURCE NATURAL SETTING AND INNER TEMPLE

In this second step of the ritual of preparation, we consciously embark on an imaginary journey, leaving the world of the rational mind to enter the inner world of the subconscious mode of functioning. Through the use of guided imagery and suggestion, we evoke the functioning of the inner senses—vision, touch, taste, smell, and hearing—to enter into an altered state of consciousness, a light trance state, in which we can gain distance from the habitual linear structure of the conscious mind.

We create, and then regularly enter into, a world of nature, of living plants and elements. In this imaginary world, where everything is organized according to our needs and desires, we find an atmosphere that is relaxing and easy to be in, where we can resource ourselves through a conscious and intuitive contact with the elements of nature present in the setting we have chosen. Restabilized by the earth, purified in water, vitalized by the air, and warmed by the Sun, we enter into contact with the elements of nature to give ourselves the qualities we need, taking time to enjoy this imaginary walk, which allows us to appreciate the qualities and beauty of nature.

Within the beauty of the natural setting, we imagine a sanctuary, a temple. A sacred place. It is to this temple that we go to enter more deeply into contact with our intuitive self. Using the imagination as a creative tool, we create the temple according to our wishes. The only criteria for creation is that this sacred space pleases us, so that, each time we go there, we feel at home, at ease and at peace, with the desire to return again.

The Resource Natural Setting and Inner Temple are utilized as triggers to switch from rational to imaginary mode, from left- to right-brain functioning, from conscious to subconscious, and as such, are essential triggers for entering into the intuitive mode. But perhaps, as importantly, these imaginary inner places serve as a protection, as a sort of buffer zone, shutting out the noise and energetic pollution of the external world, so that we can work quietly, without psychic disturbance, in our inner world.

Initially the Natural Setting and Temple are created atmospheres, brought to life by our invention and organization. However, after a time, this inner world begins to take on another dimension— a living dimension of its own. In the same way that all living nature has its rhythms and all dwellings have an atmosphere, these places can begin to transform and "speak for themselves," assisting us on our inner voyage. Given that the garden of Nature and Temple exist through our imagination, it is natural that, as we change and evolve, our needs will also evolve. Very often, these inner states of transformation can be noted through sudden changes observed in the natural setting and the Temple. Periodically, the Temple should be spring-cleaned and renovated, allowing this imaginary space to be a correct and comfortable reflection of our inner state.

Symbolically, the voyage through the Resource Natural Setting to the Temple, represents a return to the essential self that is necessary in order to have contact with the wisdom of our deeper selves. We renounce (temporarily) the external world, to embrace the inner world of our imagination, through which we rediscover our intuitive self.

It is important to take your time with this step of the ritual. You may stay as long as you like in nature, in the Temple. Use this step as part of the self-healing process of meditation and visualization. Allow yourself all the time you need to create this inner world according to your requirements. Use your imagination freely, without restraint. Think of yourself as a magician, creating your world. You are in fact doing just that!

Resource Natural Setting and Inner Temple Meditation

- Breathing gently, relaxed and aware, calm and present, close your eyes and with awareness of the flowing, gentle rhythm of your breath coming and going, become more and more settled in yourself, more and more present with each cycle of your breathing . . .

- Imagine yourself now, in a wonderful Natural Setting . . . it may be somewhere you know, it may be somewhere you imagine . . . picture this setting in your mind's eye and imagine it with all your inner senses . . . feeling the atmosphere and touching the earth, the plants, seeing the colors of nature all around you, listening to the sounds, the movements, the scents brought to you on the flowing breeze, the taste of the air . . .

- Imagine this natural scene and imagine yourself within it, the earth, water, air, Sun . . . what kind of Natural Setting is appropriate for you? . . . imagine a place that pleases you, which contains the elements of nature you love . . . how is the earth? . . . the plants, the trees? . . . is there water? . . . a lake, a river, the sea? . . .

- Allow your imagination to create a place that really pleases you, which feels nourishing to you and in which you can imagine yourself with pleasure . . . this is a special place, your special place, a sanctuary for you to go to so you can be with yourself, a place to heal, to grow, to transform, to learn . . .

- Imagine, within the sanctuary of this special Natural Setting, a Temple . . . a Temple within the Temple gardens, a sanctuary within a sanctuary, imagine a structure, a dwelling, a space totally suitable to your needs.

- It may be very simple, very elaborate . . . allow your imagination to create the vision of the perfect Temple space for you and then fill this space with furnishings and objects, with the atmosphere that appeals to you, the ambiance in which you feel at home, at ease and available to be, to relax, a space where you can install yourself, where you can meditate and contemplate and be with yourself . . .

- Taking all the time you need, let the inner vision of your Temple develop and explore the space, discovering the atmosphere . . . filling the atmosphere with your presence, making yourself at home.

- Breathing and relaxing, allow this space to nourish you. Imagine the beauty of nature that surrounds you and the wonderful atmosphere of your Temple and know that this is your special place, a healing place, a regenerating space, a place you can always come to . . . a place made just for you.

- Take several breaths, deep and full and when you feel ready, open your eyes, present and refreshed.

REALIGNMENT WITH THE VERTICAL

Having traversed the beauties of nature to install yourself (your awareness) in your inner Temple, you are naturally protected from external disturbances on both a mental and energetic level. At this point, the next step is to enter into contact with the energies of Earth and the universe as means of support, aid, and nourishment.

Realignment with the vertical describes the process of creating a conscious contact with the energies of Earth and the universe, imagining that they are beings with which you can enter into a relationship of exchange, communication, and consciousness. In the philosophy on which the intuition teachings are based, we believe in the concept of Earth and universe as Mother and Father archetypes or divinities. Earth is a being, a nourishing feminine energy, a being following her evolutionary path and experiencing her existence with a certain level of awareness, in much the same way that we experience our own. The universe for all its vastness, is also a being, intelligent, aware and in relationship with the Earth. We can enter into conscious relationship with these beings if we so choose.

The essential qualities we find when we enter into contact with the Earth are security and stability. Through the universe we find light and communion, the sense of belonging, of having a place and a purpose. By opening our awareness toward the Earth and extending our inner senses to create an energetic contact, we can find all the security and stability we need to feel safe and protected. We can imagine the Earth as Mother, offering us her abundance, the fruit and flowers of her being. Energetic contact with Earth creates a sense of grounding, of anchoring, and is achieved through breathing in the belly and becoming more present and aware in actual present time. Preoccupations with the past and future can be managed and even mastered, through the practice of regular grounding exercises and meditations, which help us to stay concentrated with our attention in the here and now. Grounding increases our aware-

Figure 9. Grounding: connecting energetically to the Earth.

ness of the experience of our physical body and our relationship with it.

To balance the density and stability of Earth, we also enter into contact with the universe, with the vastness of heaven, experienced through our perception of light and our sense of communion with existence. Extending our awareness toward heaven, we ask the light to be with us, to flow in us, to heal us. We imagine light from the universe in the form of a color and a quality of communion, and energy from Earth as a quality of stability—two energies which flow into us as a form of liquid light. The relationship with Earth and universe creates a flow of subtle energy entering through the pelvis and the crown of the head, reinforcing the vertical axis of the body. Reinforcement of the axis in this fashion gives us the balanced qualities of firmness and suppleness, stability and lightness.

Regular practice of Realignment of the Vertical eventually leads to the development of greater detachment, independence, and emotional maturity. Once we give a place to the Earth and the universe, they can begin to function for us in the subtle world of inner consciousness, communicating, guiding, and offering us their presence as a welcome accompaniment through life.

Grounding Meditation

- Imagine yourself inside your Temple, relaxed, alert, and available, present, breathing . . .

- Bring your attention to your vertebral column and imagine it as a large column of light, round, full, and firm, a column that extends from the base of your spine to the top of your head, a column of light that supports you and helps you to maintain your posture in a sitting position of meditation.

- Imagine your axis as something firm and, at the same time, supple, giving you the support you need.

Figure 10. Grounding: connecting energetically with light.

- From the base of your spine imagine the energy, the light, extends and reaches down into the earth, sending out energetic roots into the earth in much the same way that a tree grounds into the earth . . . imagine your axis extending and stabilizing, grounding you, connecting you to Earth, and from Earth energy can flow into you as a liquid light, a light of stability, of security, of presence, flowing into you from the Earth, allowing your axis to expand, and become firm and strong, stable.

- Now bring your attention to the crown of your head, and imagine your axis at this level, a column of light opening out toward the sky, opening to receive the light that flows down, that flows all around you, that flows into you through the crown of your head, bringing the qualities of lightness, of communion, the sense of belonging and of being accompanied, enfolded in light and the softness of love.

- Allow yourself to open and receive, to let the light flow in, and imagine your axis, a column of light, connected to the Earth, connected to the universe . . . open and available to receive what you need, for balance, for healing, for your well-being.

- Stay quietly for several minutes aware of your axis, breathing, being present, aware of the Earth, aware of the universe, allowing yourself to receive liquid light through the base of your spine, through the crown of your head, adding light, strength, and suppleness to your axis.

- When you feel ready, take a few deep breaths, relax your inner concentration, and open your eyes.

CENTERING IN THE HEART

Having connected energetically to the Earth and universe through the vertical axis of the subtle body, light can be distributed throughout the subtle and physical body for purification, nourishment, and balance. We imagine light as a liquid substance, clear, alive, and flowing, with the ability to flow throughout all the systems of the body.

At the same time, we shift our center of awareness from the center of the head to the chest region, imagining the heart as the center point of our consciousness, as the seat of the wisdom of the soul. The heart receives both the energy of Earth and universe—two types of liquid light that arrive, meet, and merge in the heart and, from there, circulate throughout the body as nourishing healing light.

Flowing Light Meditation

- Breathe, relax, close your eyes, and enter inside yourself. Bring you awareness to your axis and to the base of your spine, to your connection with the Earth.

- Imagine your grounding cord connecting you to the Earth and allow yourself to let go of tension, tightness, and negative thoughts, to let go of difficult emotions, letting them go down your grounding cord. Give them to the Earth as energy the Earth can recycle, letting go and relaxing, grounding.

- Giving to the Earth and also receiving from the Earth . . . imagine liquid light flowing up from the Earth, the Earth supporting you, bringing you stability, security and light . . .

- Imagine light flowing into you, through your feet, your legs, and the base of your spine, flowing in and flowing up through your axis, flowing into your chest, into your heart, breathing

Figure 11. Flowing Light Meditation: energetic light connection between belly, heart, and head.

light in, breathing tension out, being more and more available to receive the light flowing into you, flowing in, flowing up, touching you in your heart.

- Bring your attention to the universe now, the air, the sky, the Sun . . . and breathing in the air around you, imagine light flowing into you and filling you, light flowing in through the crown of your head, light flowing all around you and filling you as you breathe, clear light, white light, loving light, flowing into you, flowing through you, flowing down into your heart and filling your heart with light.

- Energy of the Earth, energy of the universe, flowing in you, filling your heart, mixing and merging within you, replenishing you with light, filling your heart with light. Breathe and accept the light flowing, filling, circulating and center yourself in your heart, Earth and universe meeting you in your heart and light flowing from your heart throughout your body.

- Relax into the feeling of yourself as a fluid, flowing being, balanced, centered, and present in your heart and, when you feel ready, let go of your inner concentration and open your eyes, taking a few full breaths.

CIRCLE OF PROTECTION

In this step of the meditation we surround ourselves in light, protecting ourselves from external energetic disturbances and creating an envelope of nourishing light that reinforces the boundaries of our subtle body.

Personal Boundary Meditation

- Breathe, ground, center, and imagine light flowing in you and around you. Be aware of your axis, and of your connection to the Earth. Grounded and centered, present and aware . . .

- Now imagine around yourself a boundary of clear, radiant light, imagine your whole body surrounded by light, a protective cocoon surrounding you, enveloping you in light, in the softness of white, flowing light.

- Imagine the boundary all around you, from above your head to below your feet, from the front of you to the back of you, from side to side . . . a personal boundary of light all around you, enveloping and protecting you, a layer of light, intelligent light, light full of the wisdom of Earth and universe, protecting you always.

- Affirm within yourself that your boundary protects you at all times, in all places, in all ways, filtering and screening the energy of life, protecting you from disturbing energy, opening up to nourishing energy. A boundary that has your best interests at heart, in all ways, always . . . .

- Imagine the boundary as an eggshell of light, with yourself comfortably centered within the boundary as a flexible, flowing, living light, adapting and changing according to your needs. Everything within the boundary is your sacred space, your inner sanctuary, your place to be centered, still and safe, nourished with light . . .

- Take a few deep breaths and, when you feel ready, open your eyes and return to normal consciousness.

ANCHORING INTUITIVE MODE

In the final step of the Ritual of Preparation, we bring all the previous steps together into one coherent meditation, at the end of which we create an anchoring of the intuitive state by connecting the thumb and index fingers at the appropriate moment when we feel well-installed in intuitive mode. Once the anchor is installed, it is used in all future meditations as a trigger reflex to bring us quickly and efficiently into intuitive mode.

Anchoring Intuitive Mode Meditation

- Become aware of your breathing and consciously choose to breathe calmly and regularly, affirming to yourself that every cycle of breath relaxes and centers you.

- Imagine yourself in your Resource Natural Setting, walking in nature . . . perceiving with your inner senses the colors, the sounds, the smells of nature, the feeling of the air caressing your skin, the sense of the ground beneath your feet as you walk through your inner landscape . . . and from this natural landscape, you arrive at your inner Temple.

- Imagine the Temple . . . your sanctuary . . . visualize the shape, the size, the position of the Temple in relation to its surroundings . . . remembering that this Temple is a special place for you, a special place for you to come to do special work . . . a place for you to be in touch with your deeper self.

- Imagine yourself inside the Temple, surrounded by furnishings and objects which help you in your purpose, imagine the colors of the walls and the furniture, the textures, the atmosphere of your Temple . . . and discover the place inside your temple that is the most appropriate place for you to sit, to

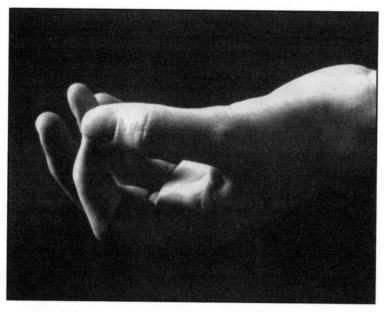

Figure 12. The Ritual of Preparation: anchoring thumb and index finger.

meditate . . . and staying in contact with the flow of your breath, coming and going, imagine yourself sitting down, comfortably installed . . .

- Bring your attention to the base of your spine, and imagine your spine as a column of light . . . extending down from the base of your spine you have light energy that penetrates deeply into the Earth . . . a column of light connecting you to the Earth . . . a grounding cord of light going down deeply and strongly into the Earth.

- Affirm your connection with the Earth . . . "I am here, in my body and the Earth is here with me. I connect with the Earth." Imagine the Earth sending nourishment to you . . . a stream of liquid light flowing to you from the Earth . . . a light flowing up into your body through the base of your spine . . . a light flowing into your chest and from your chest, a liquid light flowing through your body, bringing nourishment and support from the Earth to you . . . drawing the energy of the Earth into you . . . with every cycle of your breath, being present, relaxed, available, and aware of how you feel, aware of your inner state.

- Now bring your attention to the crown of your head and imagine light flowing toward you from the immensity of the universe . . . from a source of great love, light comes to you . . . this light is a clear, white light and the light flows into you . . . a liquid light flowing into you through your head and down into your chest to your heart . . . being available to receive the nourishment you need from the universe, light from the universe flowing into you and filling you, flowing through you . . .

- The light of the Earth and the light of the universe, mixing in you and flowing through you . . . bringing you balance and harmony, bringing you the qualities of energy you need to be well, to be balanced . . .

- Imagine yourself filling with light . . . light fills you and overflows all around you . . . the light falls all around your body . . . and imagine yourself enfolded in light. Light from the Earth and light from the universe flowing in you, enfolding you, surrounding you softly . . .

- Affirm within yourself the words of your Eternal Key, feeling within yourself the meaning that these words have for you. Be aware of what happens within you when you repeat this sentence several times . . . with every cycle of your breathing staying centered and present . . .

- Very gently bring your thumb and index finger together in a firm but soft pressure, creating an anchor, an easy and simple access to your intuitive mode . . . Affirm within yourself . . . "I am a clear channel for truth," and "My intuitive self is alive in me." Imagine your intuitive self as an aspect of you . . . alive, present, available . . . you can ask questions of this aspect of yourself and receive answers that are clear and correct . . . answers that guide you and help you in your life . . . answers that may come as feelings, images, or messages . . .

- Being present, available, aware, in touch with yourself, aware of your inner state . . . breathing, energy flowing, light circulating, present and centered within the tranquillity of your Temple . . .

- When you feel ready, take several deep breaths, open your eyes and return to the external world.

• • •

From now on, always use this finger/thumb anchoring every time you wish to enter into your intuitive mode. As soon as you close your eyes and begin to breathe calmly and regularly, connect your finger and thumb in the same fashion, ensuring that you will enter simply and deeply into your intuitive mode of being.

4

UTILIZING YOUR
INTUITION

CHAPTER TWELVE

The Creative Cycle of Intuitive Expression

Discovery, exploration, and utilization of the intuition is essentially an inner journey, a journey of awareness, which requires time, attention, and an internal state of discernment and lucidity. It is, in a sense, a journey without end, without destination; an inward voyage that presents seemingly endless horizons of possibilities. The discovery and development of the inner senses leads us, quite naturally, to a deeper contact with ourselves and with the richness of our inner world. Reunited with our more essential self, in touch with the ebb and flow of our inner rhythms of being, life takes on a different perspective and we begin to regard ourselves with more acceptance, understanding, and self-love.

The inner opening and the reconciliation of the heart and soul, which is the fruit of the development of the intuition, follows a pathway that is unique to every individual who embarks on the journey. The insights and revelations discovered along the way come in many forms and sizes, each adding its own dimension to the transformation of the voyager. Given the unique nature of every person and the variety of ways in which the intuition can express itself, it can be surprising to learn that, in fact, the intuition follows a very orderly path in its function and expression. More correct, perhaps, to say that the intuition needs an orderly path, an organized inner structure through which to manifest, so that it may function accurately and reliably.

Whenever the intuitive function is put into play, a specific sequence of events should be followed in the body/being to allow the intuition to express itself to its full potential. As in all creative processes, there is a movement of conception, gestation, and birth; a complete cycle in which each step is a prerequisite for the one following. The cycle of intuitive functioning follows five fundamental and essential stages in its creative expression.

PERSONAL PREPARATION

The first and most important stage in the intuitive process is the time taken for personal inner preparation. It is essential to temporarily cease external activities and to create a quiet space in which to withdraw, both symbolically and actually, from the outside world. In this initial phase, we take the time to come back to ourselves, by breathing quietly and following all the steps of the ritual of preparation in the form of a self-guided meditation:

- Respiration, relaxation, awareness
- Resource Natural Setting
- Inner Temple
- Realignment with the vertical: axis
- Grounding—Earth/universe
- Flowing energy
- Circle of Protection
- Anchoring intuitive mode

ENTERING INTO INTUITIVE MODE

Once we have accessed intuitive mode by following the preceding steps, we take several moments to go even more deeply into the inner state of still, empty calm, verifying that we are well centered, present, and aware. At this point, it is possible to ask questions, request information, and seek guidance from the intuitive self. It is imperative that all questions be posed clearly and precisely, and that information sought have a real sense, a coherent value. The more we approach the intuition with respect, the same quality of respect we would offer to a wise and sacred being, the more the intuition can respond with this same quality of sacred respect.

RECEIVING RESPONSES

Once the question has been posed, it is necessary to stay quietly available, receptive, and patient, allowing the intuition to seek and supply the correct response to our query. Sometimes, the response will come quickly, almost simultaneous with the question. Often, however, especially in the beginning, some moments, even some minutes, may be needed before we begin to feel the response welling up inside our inner awareness. At this moment, we must pay attention to sensations, feelings, words, and images which stream through our consciousness, allowing our inner senses to bring us the answers to the information we have demanded. We stay neutral, without judgment, patient and receptive, as impression builds upon impression, giving us a clear sense and a holistic response to the question posed.

INTERPRETATION OF INFORMATION

Having received information from our intuition, we need to clarify the information, re-asking questions internally to verify and cross-check any impressions we have received that we may feel seem contradictory or confusing. At this point, we also check for projections and for rational-mind interference, discarding those impressions which cause us to hesitate, asking, internally, that only correct information remains in our conscious awareness, and letting go of any false impressions not relevant to the question.

We ask our intuitive self to help us to integrate the meaning of the response given, so that it has a sense for us. Internally receptive, we stay present and available to understand the symbolic message given to us by our intuition and its relevance to the question posed. After some moments of waiting, we understand and can interpret the significance of the impressions received.

COMMUNICATION/EXPRESSION

In this phase of intuitive function, we express the information, either by communicating and sharing with another, or as a concrete action grounded in reality that brings the intuitive process to a state of realization. It is essential in this stage that there is an external action, whether through words or physical movement, that allows the creative intuitive process to find its place in the material world of thought and form.

CHAPTER THIRTEEN

Guidelines for Interpreting the Symbolism of Intuition

When we enter into our intuitive mode of being and pose questions to this aspect of ourselves, a response is always forthcoming. As inner teacher, the intuitive self assumes her role with great commitment, responsibility, and presence. If we find that the question is not answered, it is not because our inner teacher is not on the job, it is because we have not adjusted our inner antennae sufficiently to hear, see, feel, or otherwise perceive the response she has given.

It can be extremely helpful to imagine the intuitive self as a being, a being with a purpose and with the means to realize that purpose. Even though, in reality, your intuitive aspect is actually you, your true being, imagining your intuitive self with a particular face, body, and voice will help you to enter into contact and communicate more easily.

The means through which intuitive self will realize her purpose is your body/mind, your physical vehicle in this world. Thanks to the physical body, your soul can gather the experience it needs to evolve and develop to its full capacity. Thanks to the interrelation between your soul and your conscious and subconscious mind (and their relation to your physical body), your intuition can communicate its perceptions through your inner senses. The body can then provide the intuition with criteria for evaluation through your physical senses and their contact with your external environment.

We must always remember that the body and soul, intuition and mind, are in fact one unit, functioning as a whole, as a global operation. It is for this reason that we are somewhat prone to commit errors of perception, even when we utilize the function of our intuition. It is difficult to isolate the many different parts of ourselves, defining exactly which part does what, in which sequence, in relation to which other function. For learning purposes, we isolate and identify the different aspects of the intuitive sequence so that our functioning can be understood more clearly. However, it is imperative to retain the essential sense of ourselves as a whole being, a synthesis of physical/spiritual, intuitive/rational, body/mind, and personality/soul.

A well-developed intuition that functions in a manner disassociated from the context of its application, is not a terribly useful intuition, as it lacks a coherent link with the existing reality. Therefore, it cannot be very beneficial in a practical sense, in either the short or long term. Intuition functions beyond the linear rational-mind concepts of space/time and of mental logic. For this reason, intuitive messages are most often perceived through dreamlike transmissions, received in "awake dream" trance states of meditational awareness. A personal work of inner preparation is an essential prerequisite before we can begin to receive clear information, answers to our questions, and unsolicited guidance.

Once we begin to receive transmissions from our intuitive self, we will need to be able to interpret the messages received—to decipher the meaning contained within the symbolic response to the question that has been posed. Interpretation is an art in itself, an apprenticeship demanding time, patience, lucidity, and lots of margin for error, especially in the beginning. Because of the potential traps of power, manipulation, and illusion that are always present when we utilize our intuition, intermediary methods relying strongly on intuitive capacity, such as astrology, tarot, pendulum, I Ching, and numerology, have found a considerable place in the world of esoteric and spiritual counseling. In these techniques, the planets, the cards, and the numbers are the principal symbolic tools with which the practitioner works. The symbols are interpreted in relation to themselves and their interrelationship with each other.

Protected by the familiarity of a known symbolic structure through which to work, the practitioner is less "personally" involved, therefore less prone (theoretically) to project, manipulate, and interpret incorrectly. With pure intuitive work, there are no cards, planets, or numbers. The tool with which we work is ourselves; our intuitive self. Because of this fact, it is not realistic to imagine we can be totally objective. Our very perception of reality is subjective and always will be, even when we are centered, detached from our personality, and securely installed in intuitive mode. The intuitive self is a seeker of truth and it is this essential search for truth that helps us go beyond our subjective interpretation of the nature of reality and arrive at a relatively objective perception of the truths existing in front of us. In searching for the truth of ourselves, we discover who we are and also deliver ourselves from the illusions of who we are not. Even though we have a remarkable capacity for self-deception and self-delusion, our innate capacity to seek and sense the truth is an ability that takes predominance if we allow and encourage it to do so.

It is virtually impossible to provide absolute rules for interpreting the symbolism found through the function of the intuition. Not only would it be too simplistic, too rigid, and inadequate, it would also be unethical. There are two major factors involved in this reasoning. In the world of intuitive function, no truth is absolute. Truth is truth, but truth is always relative—relative to the person, the situation, the moment, and the context of the question/problem/preoccupation that we are exploring. Similarly, intuition exists beyond space and time. Therefore, what is true in one moment, may or may not be true in the next moment. We must always stay open to a spontaneous understanding of the significance of a symbolic transmission, without the interference of the rational mind attempting to classify and compartmentalize the symbol according to information received in another moment.

What we discover when we go beyond rational and moral frameworks of preconceived ideas pertaining to the nature of reality is that existence is in constant movement and human beings are (or can be if they allow it) in a constant process of change and evolution. We can perceive that every human being has a movement and this movement is appropriate for them, is, in fact, the reflection of the truth of their being, the truth of their soul. In a moral sense, there is no right or wrong, there is simply the movement—the movement toward creation, toward destruction, toward life, death, and rebirth. Nobody is wrong. Everybody is right. Everybody always has a reason for each of their actions. Every soul is in the process of learning something, through each and every one of their actions, whether they know that consciously or not.

For this reason, interpretation is a delicate subject, complicated to learn, because of the necessary lack of absolute rules, and complicated to teach for the same reason. What I may call interpretation could easily be experienced by another as judgment and by another as truth.

To function beyond the limiting nature of judgment, we are obliged to put social and moral beliefs aside, just as we put our rational mind aside when we prepare ourselves to enter into intuitive mode.

There are, however, guidelines which can help us to interpret the symbolism of the intuition as it functions through the body/mind. A symbol is usually something we see—an image. An image is composed of shapes and colors which combine to give the image a form that we can describe with words. Within the form, we find an atmosphere, a feeling. Feeling leads us to emotion, and emotion leads us to our bodies, to the world of sensation, texture, and physical touch.

It is through following this progression—images, words, feeling, sensations—that we can interpret symbolic information received by the intuition.

Because of the subtle nature of intuition, it is a function more naturally aligned to the medium of images, which are also subtle and fine in nature. Intuition begins, in a sense, in the head, in an awareness of the consciousness. From there, it journeys toward the world of physical matter through the media of words, feelings, and sensations.

If we begin with an image, we intuitively "step into" the image with our consciousness, describing what we see with words and feelings, touching the atmosphere within the image with our inner senses. Through this intuitive interaction with the image, in which we are engaged with all our senses, we perceive the meaning of the image in relation to the question/problem with which we are working.

Ultimately, it is just as possible to proceed in the other direction—i.e., sensation, feeling, words, image. In body-centered psychotherapies, this approach is widely used to guide people toward intuitive insights and healing integrations. We locate a sensation in the body and become more and more aware of it, "going inside" and exploring the shape and texture of the sensation until we feel the atmosphere. The atmosphere puts us in touch with the associated emotion. Very often, once we begin to express the emotion (with sounds and words), we begin to experience images connected to the original sensation. The images may be connected to our past or present life. Once the images are explored, expressed, and integrated, we find ourselves more in touch, more connected, to the truth of who we are. Returning to the original sensation, we find it has transformed and we are more at ease in that part of our body than when we began the exercise.

In the work of intuitive perception, it can be more difficult to begin at the level of sensation and progress toward the level of images, as this is the most "dense" level of perception, as well as the most "personal," the most physical. For most of us it is easier to enter an image with our awareness than it is to penetrate into a physical sensation, especially if the sensation is an unpleasurable one.

The advantage of images is that we have some distance to begin with—"I am here and the image is there. I can go toward the image with my consciousness." With sensations, we have greater difficulty keeping our sense of distance. To feel a sensation we must go into it and, once we are absorbed into the realm of sensation, it can be difficult to differentiate between self, the other, and the sensation itself.

As we become more advanced in intuitive practice, we become more adept at working in and around the perimeters of sensation/image. We develop intuitive flexibility, learning to move our awareness with fluidity through the worlds of image, feeling, and sensation, seeking information and receiving verification from several sources, so that we can be more certain of the truth of the interpretations we give to the information received.

In the beginning, this process of seeking, investigating, and verifying information seems very complicated and sophisticated and well beyond our capacities. With practice we begin to grasp the technique and slowly develop a capacity of intuitive flexibility that permits us to travel with our awareness beyond space/time/matter limits, into the inner world of our being and the world of others with whom we practice and work.

When you ask a question of your intuition, you receive an answer, given either as an image, words, feeling, sensation, or as a combination of all these. It is imperative that, when you go into trance and before you begin asking questions, you take stock of yourself and of your own physical, emotional, and inner state. Knowing how you are before beginning a session gives you a frame of reference within which to work. It is especially useful to observe all physical sensations—"butterflies" in the belly, pain in the solar plexus, headache, pain behind the shoulder blades—as well as the emotional state—nervous, afraid, a bit depressed. It is very possible that, during the session, your own personal state will transform completely. Very often, it will transform for the better, though occasionally you will feel worse after a session. This is because the movement of entering into yourself more deeply propels you more deeply into the experience of your problems before it delivers you from them through the movement of transformation and healing.

Once you have taken stock of your actual state, you are ready to begin asking questions and receiving information and responses. When you ask a question of your intuition, you must be willing to wait patiently for the response, which will come in its own time. At times, it comes very quickly, but sometimes you may have to repeat the demand, clarifying your request or perhaps stating it in a different way. You must let your intuition know what it is you want. If you are vague about what you want, you will have the tendency to receive vague information. Using your intuition is like being a detective— you ask questions, more questions, and even more questions, until you have the answers that satisfy you; answers that give you the feeling you have, at last, discovered the truth.

In the beginning of a session, as you are still entering into your deep trance state, you may have the impression of receiving lots of seemingly disassociated images which can be vague, cloudy, even strange. In this case, take your time and wait until you feel really ready to begin before actually starting. If, once you feel well centered, you ask a question and receive an image that seems disassociated in some way from the question, simply ask the image to disappear and start again. In this case, if the image was disassociated from the question, it will not come back. If the image is the correct image, given to you by your intuition, it will reappear and this will be a sign for you to proceed with this image as your departure point for the work you are doing. An image given to you by your intuition will not require an effort on your part to maintain. An image created by your mind, by your imagination, will demand an inner effort to maintain. If you feel yourself engaged in an inner effort to "create and tell the story," let go of the effort, stop, and begin again quietly, waiting patiently for your intuition to begin to do its work.

Once you have an image that you feel is appropriate, you can begin to explore it in more depth. Essentially, the process of interpretation of a symbolic image requires that you ask of your intuitive self internally "What do you mean?"; "What does that mean?"; "What does this mean?" Ask until you feel you understand the meaning for yourself in a tangible sense, so you can move on to the next question and image.

It is essential to trust the information and impressions you receive during the session. If you are working with an image and suddenly begin to feel sleepy, anxious, joyful, nauseous, tense, or sad, you can be sure that these feelings and sensations are connected to the image and are therefore important pieces of information coming to you from your intuition. These experiences help you to interpret the symbolic image, but you must allow yourself to make the connection. Do not preoccupy yourself with reflections about the possibility of projections. Simply go ahead and trust.

When you receive a symbolic image, begin by describing the image in as much detail as possible. "Zoom in" on the image and describe it with your internal voice and/or your spoken voice. Explore and describe the image and slowly allow yourself to open more and more to the image; begin to feel the atmosphere of your perception. Each time you perceive something, ask your intuition to tell you the meaning, the significance, of what you are perceiving. Pay attention to the aspects of the image to which you feel particularly drawn, the aspects that capture your attention and seem to reach out to you. Be aware that the image is a symbolic message but that this message has a relationship to concrete reality. The real art of interpretation lies in the ability to take a relatively abstract image and/or feeling and associate it in a lucid and concrete fashion to daily life. If you can translate the symbolic images in this manner, the transmissions you receive from your intuition will take on a tangible meaning and have a concrete impact within your daily life.

Let's take an example to demonstrate more clearly the steps of interpretation.

• *Case Study* •

I ask my intuition to give me the image of a tree that represents my actual state of being.

I see a tree in a glade in the forest. A tall, slender, graceful tree with sil-ver bark, lots of leaves, small and very green. The tree is next to a brook, in a meadow full of spring flowers. There is a breeze blowing gen-tly—the grass and flowers are swaying, insects are buzzing, birds are singing. It's a summer scene. The water is flowing, bubbling along. Everything is alive, full of color. Next to this tree is another tree, a sturdy pine, solid, strong, healthy, with lots of presence. It is very close to "my" tree, providing support, companionship, and sharing the water and light of nature. It is, however, crowding the space a little. The first tree wants to move, to dance, to sway, and cannot, simply because the other tree is a little too close.

Entering into the image, to feel the atmosphere, I am aware of the beauty of the scene—it is tranquil and alive and at the same time, peace-ful and joyful, with a feeling of communication, interrelation, and shar-ing. I feel the comfort of the two trees sharing the space, of how my tree loves to have the other close by but how, at the same time, it is a little crowded . . . as though the two trees had grown a lot, and now there is a problem of space. I see the second tree leaning toward the first and reach-ing for the light, reaching for the water. I feel that the trees need more space, more freedom, more independence but at the same time, they need to maintain their unique connection.

I imagine I create more space so the first tree can breathe, sway, dance . . . and as soon as I imagine that, I feel different in my body. I feel more present in my legs, more free in my arms; I feel movement in my belly. I imagine I ask the other tree to move back a little bit, to connect to its own light source, so my tree can receive the Sun more directly. The second tree moves willingly, allowing the Sun to bathe my tree in its warmth. I feel recharged. I feel joyful. The other tree is beside me, sharing, and we both have more space, more breathing space.

The interpretation I give to this image I have received:

Overall, I am well. My environment suits me, I have my place, but I lack movement, I feel inhibited, I cannot express the fullness of my inner dimension because I need more space, more light. (This information was received in the month of January, during the European winter and I remember very well how I felt the need to breathe, to be outside and reconnect to the Sun and my own inner movement. I was also needing to move my body and circulate my energy.)

• • •

When you receive an image and begin to describe it, the image very often takes on a life of its own and becomes a moving image, like an unfolding film scenario. You ask objects within the image to speak to you and, on an intuitive level, they answer your questions and explain their significance in relation to the question/problem.

If you receive information from your intuition and you find you do not understand the sense of it, even though you may have questioned and received further clarification, simply stop trying to understand for the moment and just stay aware of the information. Very often, we need time to integrate and eventually understand messages from our intuition. It is not always necessary to interpret, or even to understand consciously, the images we have been given. It is enough to have the image and to allow the image to go to work within us on a more subconscious level.

The art of interpretation is a subtle art, demanding communication between the intuition and the rational mind, as well as imagination and diplomacy. The marriage between mind and intuition is a sacred movement of reconciliation between body and soul, between the masculine and feminine aspects of ourselves. A sacred movement of this type takes time and demands patience and awareness. Every time you use your intuition, you are working toward this reconciliation within yourself.

CHAPTER FOURTEEN

Personal Meditation Practice and Techniques for Evolution

Meditation is an intrinsic part of the spiritual path and its importance cannot be overestimated in the development of the intuition. Meditation is the practice of inner contemplation that creates an internal atmosphere of availability and awareness through which the intuition can function. In simple terms, we can describe the process of meditation as "coming home to oneself." Meditation exercises form the basis of most spiritual teachings and, even though the form of the exercises may seem unlimited, the fundamental purpose of meditation is essentially the same, i.e., to help us to be centered, present, and quiet within ourselves.

Meditation is a journey of reconciliation with self, of reintegration. For this reason, we can call it a "homecoming." Essentially, meditation is simple. We sit, we quiet ourselves, and we *are* ourselves, with ourselves, maintaining awareness of what happens during the period of sitting. While meditating, we "work" on ourselves with light, energy, and love, repairing and healing our bodies and spirits as we go. For a process so essentially simple, the results can be astounding, especially when we practice regularly. We almost always feel better after a session of meditation. We are more centered, more present, more loving, more clear, and more available. So why is it so difficult to find the time, the place, the moment, to do it? Something that is so good for us . . . why do we resist it so?

We resist because of the power and presence of the rational mind. We resist because of our ancient belief systems. We resist because we have a long-established habit, anchored in our daily lives, of not giving to ourselves the quality of attention we really need to be well, centered, and reconciled with ourselves. Meditation is not a process that needs to endure a long time to be beneficial, but it does need to be practiced regularly. Better to meditate for ten minutes every day, than for one hour every week, but, ultimately, one hour every week is a great improvement over a four-hour endurance marathon once a month.

Fundamentally, all spiritual paths are personal disciplines involving choice and decision. Without meditation, the path loses its definition, its clarity, and its presence in our lives. There is always a choice, but when it comes to the question of meditation, we must eventually realize that it is imperative to create the time and space to meditate regularly. If we don't, we lose the benefits already gained and slowly lose our sense of purpose in having begun in the first place.

The most common mental behavioral trap and rationalization for not meditating it is that, when we feel well, we think we don't need it; we're too busy feeling well and being creative. When we feel bad and we know we need it, we can't do it because we feel too bad to concentrate—it's too much effort, we'll only feel worse if we do it, it's not worth it, etc. We can always find reasons not to meditate. Meditation is something like physical exercise and good eating habits. We know we should do it, but do we? The only solution to this dilemma that I have found is to eliminate the question of choice and raise the problem to the level of an imperative. After a while the habit becomes ingrained in life and we can experience meditation as a healthy habit, with the same appreciated value as sleeping, sunshine, breathing, exercise, good food, and clean water.

I personally believe that one hour of meditation each day is a reasonable amount of time to devote to the inner work of looking after ourselves in the silence of our inner temple. You will find very often in meditation that you need at least several minutes just to become truly quiet and then an additional thirty minutes to benefit from the stillness and to go further into the deepness of yourself.

Even though meditation is, in essence, a simple process, it is not always easy to practice. Do not expect a session to be easy and, above all, do not think meditation is something you will master after several sessions. Meditation is a life discipline, a life journey, and an inner exploration of the great mystery of discovering who you really are. All the great spiritual traditions of the world insist on the importance and ultimate value of meditation. You cannot, realistically, escape meditation. You can change the spiritual school, you can change the technique, but you cannot change the truth. The truth is that, if you wish to transform and evolve, if you wish to heal yourself, you have to begin by sitting down, closing your eyes, breathing, and becoming still and available to yourself, to be with yourself.

The personal meditation practices that follow have been arranged in a progressive order that I encourage you to follow, especially in the beginning. With the sixteen meditations presented here, you will have enough possibilities for months and months of personal inner work. I have been working with these meditations and variations thereof for over fifteen years, in groups, trainings, and personal inner work and they always provide me with material for contemplation and inner movement. Do not make the mistake of thinking you constantly have to learn new meditations in order to feel you are progressing. A variety of different meditation possibilities is interesting for the mind and appetizing for the spirit, in the same fashion that a changing diet is interesting in the routine of food preparation. But we must remember that too much change can lead to dispersion and superficiality.

The meditations that you find the most difficult to practice are most likely the meditations that you most need to do. If this is the case, try to persevere and trust that you are progressing, even when you feel blocked, lost, and without hope. It is not uncommon in the inner work of meditation to experience difficulties during a moment which is leading up to a major breakthrough in consciousness. When the going gets rough, keep on going! Do not give up. Remember that a true healing is preceded by a healing crisis—a crisis necessary so that true healing can occur. Awareness of blockages is a sacred awareness, and evidence of progress. Above all, continue!

Practice regularly and trust that every time you meditate you are, in fact, contributing to the development of your intuition.

REGULAR MAINTENANCE PROGRAM

The regular maintenance program is exactly that—meditations to practice regularly, to keep you "in shape." These two meditations ensure that, on an inner level, you stay open and connected with yourself, so that your intuition can function for you. These meditations also help to keep the channels open between your rational and intuitive mind, allowing you to maintain flexibility between your inner and outer worlds.

Ritual of Preparation

In this meditation, the steps of the ritual of preparation are used to create the inner structure through which we can welcome the presence of our intuitive being into our consciousness.

Recommended time: 15 to 30 minutes.

- Sit, close your eyes and bring your attention to your breathing, finding a rhythm of breathing that is calming and relaxing.

- During several cycles of respiration, simply be aware of your breathing, becoming more and more present, more and more with yourself, with each cycle of breathing. Be aware of how you feel, of your mood, of thoughts coming and going and be in a state of acceptance of yourself.

- Imagine yourself in your beautiful Resource Natural Setting, surrounded by all the beauties of nature that are resourcing for you and allow yourself to perceive nature with your inner senses, absorbing into you the beneficial qualities of nature as you wander through the landscape you have imagined. After a time, you arrive at your inner Temple and you enter inside, appreciating the atmosphere of peace and harmony, of balance, that you find each time you visit your Temple. You install yourself comfortably, aware of the breath coming and going, present with yourself, present and relaxed.

- Bringing your attention to the spinal column, imagine your body as a vertical column of light, firm and supple, wide and long, a column of light extending down into the Earth, grounding you, connecting you to the Earth, allowing you to release tension from your body to give to the Earth.

- Imagine light from the universe flowing into you through the crown of your head, flowing and circulating in you, flowing into your heart and flowing through you, energy of Earth, energy of universe, flowing in you, filling you and circulating through your body as a river of light.

- Imagine your body is surrounded by a sphere of light, a sphere of protection and, within the circle of light, within the boundary of your sacred space, you can be with yourself, secure and stable, present, breathing, receiving what you need from the Earth, receiving what you need from the sky, for balance, for healing, for being with yourself.

- Anchor your finger and thumb and affirm within yourself, "My intuitive self is alive within me." Be aware of energy and light circulating within your physical and subtle body and stay centered and present within yourself.

- When you feel ready, gently bring yourself back to everyday consciousness.

No-mind Meditation

This is a meditation of not-doing, not-thinking, not-acting.
Recommended time: 20 to 45 minutes.

- Follow the steps of the ritual of preparation.

- Anchor the thumb and finger together and affirm within yourself, "I am. I simply am. Being is enough." From time to time, you may repeat these sentences internally. Be aware of sensations, feelings, thoughts, and images that come and go and detach yourself, distance yourself from all attachment to these occurrences which happen.

- Imagine yourself as a vast, blue sky and imagine that sensations, feelings, and thoughts are simply clouds, appearing and disappearing, coming and going.

- Breathe and be aware of your breath as a movement coming and going, like thoughts coming and going, and be available within yourself to disappear into the stillness of no-mind, the calm of simply being, present, detached, still, and quiet. Do not try to create or change your state. Do not follow the white clouds that come and go. Simply be. "I am. I simply am. Being is enough."

- When you feel ready, gently bring yourself back to everyday consciousness and stretch and relax your body.

CURRENT STATE OF BEING

These meditations are particularly useful as intuitive information-gathering exercises that can be followed by meditations for self-healing. In meditations such as these, your intuition is free to function on a very rich, symbolic level. It is important that you allow the images you receive to "speak to you," so that you can better understand the meanings contained within the richness of the symbols. If the images "wobble," come and go, or seem absolutely strange to you, you may banish them and ask your intuition to give you symbolic images that are correct and true for you. If the same images reappear, accept them and work with them, even though they may seem strange or mysterious. With time the meaning and message contained within the images will probably become clear to you.

Tree Meditation

Recommended time: 20 to 30 minutes.

- Prepare yourself by following all the steps of the ritual of preparation.

- When you feel ready, anchored in intuitive mode, centered, present, and clear, ask your intuitive self to present you with the image of a tree which represents your actual state of being.

- You may imagine the tree appears on the intuitive screen just in front of your eyes, or you may imagine you are walking in nature and you discover this tree . . . The tree that you perceive may be like an actual tree or it may be a very symbolic, very imaginary tree. Accept the tree that your intuition presents to you and begin to explore it with your intuitive awareness. Regard it from a distance, observing its size, its shape, and its silhouette. Become aware of the environment in which the tree is located . . . on a hill? in a forest? all alone? next to water? Perceive the general environment of the tree, asking your intuitive self how the tree is connected to the four elements, to the earth, water, air, and fire. Imagine you can examine the earth in which tree is planted. Is it rich and nourishing? Or not? Does the tree receive all the water it needs? Is the air clean and pure? Does the tree have access to all the sunshine it needs? Explore the tree . . . the trunk, the branches, the leaves, the roots . . . In what state do you find the tree? How is the grounding? How are the leaves of the tree? How do you find the posture of the tree? What type of atmosphere does this tree have? How do you feel in your body when you perceive the tree? How do you feel emotionally? What do you notice about this tree that is particularly interesting, unusual, striking?

- Allow your intuition to guide you to explore the symbolic image of this tree. Do not begin to think about the tree or the fact that it represents you. Just explore the tree with your inner senses, with your intuitive self and absorb all the impressions you receive.

- Ask your intuition to communicate with you, to tell you what the tree lacks . . . grounding, water, Sun, air, company, a view . . . ? ask about what the tree needs for healing . . . relocation, pruning, clean air, postural adjustment . . . ?

- When you have received the responses to your questions, allow the image of the tree to fade, continue to meditate quietly for a few minutes, and then gently return to normal consciousness.

Write down, or even better, do a drawing of the tree you have intuitively perceived. What is the message here for you about your current state of being?

• • •

The image of the tree as a reflection of the human being is a particularly rich and touching symbol with which to work. In the tree we find a simplified version of ourselves. The trunk of the tree represents our spine and general body, the roots represent our feet and grounding ability, and the leaves represent our relationship with the universe and light. The environment relates to the environment in which we live on a daily basis. The quality of the earth speaks to us about the fundamental nourishing quality of our everyday existence—the quality of the food we eat, the work we do, the place we live. The presence or lack of adequate water indicates the quality of emotional nourishment we experience in our lives. Too much water can be as damaging as not enough, and changes may need to be made to find the balance, to find the correct dose. The quality of air is related to mental stimulation, movement, and change. Not enough air, or polluted air, can indicate that the environment is not suitable for mental growth and intellectual creativity because of a stifling effect. Too much air (a strong breeze or wind), can indicate a lack of protection, overexposure, and the need to create a more sheltered environment where the energies are less dispersed. The presence or absence of Sun relates to the quality of spiritual nourishment in life.

After practicing this meditation, it can be useful to spend some time out in nature, giving yourself actual contact with the elements of nature of which you have perceived a need, replenishing yourself by simply being present in the atmosphere of the corresponding elements.

• *Case Study* •

I see a tree on top of a round hill, a fruit tree in flower, with a view all around. A tree well-placed and proud, pleased to be a tree. There is plenty of Sun, and a lot of wind. The wind is blowing in gusts and the tree has difficulty staying grounded and stable with all the wind blowing. At the same time, the tree loves the wind—the wind is very present, a loving presence; but it is a bit too powerful. The tree finds the presence of the wind exciting and reacts as though being tickled roughly. Every time the tree is tickled, it loses its grounding and becomes more and more exposed to the air at the level of its roots. The feeling is one of instability and over-stimulation. The tree needs protection, a more moderate wind, and deeper and more stable grounding.

House Meditation

Recommended time: 30 to 40 minutes.

- Prepare yourself by following all the steps of the ritual of preparation. When you feel ready, anchor yourself into intuitive mode and ask your intuition to show you the image of a house that represents, symbolically, your current state of being. Let the image of the house appear and, with your intuitive awareness, explore the exterior of the house in detail. Observe the location of the house, and the shape and size of the house, its color and atmosphere. Perceive the roof, the walls, the windows and imagine the state of the foundations of the house. Do not think about the fact that this house represents you, simply allow the house to be there and use your intuition to perceive and explore it.

- Find the doorway through which you can enter the house; prepare yourself to enter. Inside the house, you will find four rooms representing your physical, emotional, mental, and spiritual state.

- Find yourself in front of the door marked physical state, take a breath, and enter the room, being available within yourself to perceive the symbolic images you discover in this room.

Explore the room, feel the atmosphere and allow yourself to take all the time you need to absorb the ambiance of this space. Notice the objects, the furnishings, the colors . . . be aware of other presences in the room. Be aware of how you feel within yourself as you explore this room. Do you feel well in this space? Are you in harmony with the atmosphere? Does the room appeal to you? If not, what bothers you? What would you like to change? How would you prefer it to be different? Simply become aware of your feelings in relation to the room, and of your preferences, and, when you are ready, leave the room of your physical state, closing the door behind you.

- Next, you will find yourself in front of the door of your emotional state. Repeat the experience with the room of the emotional state and then with the rooms of the mental and the spiritual states.

- When you have explored the four rooms, leave the house and find yourself back in your Temple. Take a few minutes to meditate quietly in your Temple, contemplating the information you have received about the four levels of your being. Simply be aware of this information, accepting, and not struggling to understand or analyze.

- Thank your intuition for its presence in your life and, when you feel ready, come out of your meditative state.

While the Tree Meditation allows you to gain a perspective of yourself in relation to the Earth, universe, and the environment you function in, the House Meditation gives you insights into your inner state of being and the way you are in relationship to yourself. Both meditations can provide you with a wealth of material to work with for self-healing and transformation. Even if you do not rationally understand the signification of a symbolic image, you can feel, through your physical reaction and emotional state, whether you are at ease or not with any particular image. With the lucidity of intuitive perception, you can gain valuable insights into the structure and nature of your inner world and with the insights gained, you can more deeply understand yourself and your true needs.

• Case Study •

I see a house, a wooden villa, nestled in the garden of a tropical landscape. Trees and flowers and plants everywhere, a soft, fragrant breeze blowing, warm air, lots of light, but also shade from all the tropical Sun. The house is open, with a veranda, curtains softly blowing in the breeze, and there are comfortable cane chairs on the veranda, with cushions in bright colors. There are wind chimes singing. There is a cat, sprawled and sleeping on the wooden floor in a shaded place. The atmosphere is alive, peaceful, clean, open, and very welcoming.

I go into the room of the physical and I see a room of wood, like a sauna room, almost empty, except for a beautiful Persian rug on the floor in colors of deep red, cream, and rich, rich blue. The rug is big and thick, luxurious. On the walls there are wooden shelves and here and there are objects of art—vases, bowls, crystals. It is very simple. There is a fireplace with a big fire burning and I see myself in front of the fire, back to the door, staring into the fire in a very contemplative mood. I am happy to be alone. I do not wish to be disturbed. The fire is what I need and in front of it is where I want to be. The fire (red + heat) is healing me.

I go to the room of the emotional and I find a room lacking light. There is a deep carpet and a big, old table. On the table is writing material and nothing else. The room is virtually empty, except for the table, and seems stuffy and uninhabited. It is not appealing to me at all. What is the writing material doing there? Why is it so dark? I do not feel at ease with what I perceive here. I do not feel like spending much time in this space. It is like a room from a monastery—austere, cold, businesslike (not at all like me on an emotional level!).

I go to the room of the mental and here I find a huge library, full of books. It is an old, ancient library, very well organized, everything in its place, with tables to sit and work at and reference cards at my fingertips. It is very quiet, very peaceful, and I feel well in the atmosphere. I have the feeling that, if I need something, I can always find it. Everything is filed away correctly and the space is clean, well lit, and well cared for. I feel at home here. I will come back. But why is my writing equipment in the emotional room and not here?

I continue my exploration, going now to the room of the spiritual. Going through the door, I find a landscape of flowing water, a small, sandy white beach, and a green grassy place with flowers and birds. There is a canoe and I see myself taking journeys in the canoe along the waterways, going far out onto the rivers, disappearing into the mist, coming back later and resting in the Sun on the bank of the river with the warm, white sand warming my body. There is the feeling of going far away to visit mysterious places, places I must go alone, for there is only place for one person in my little canoe. There is a somewhat solitary atmosphere, at the same time peaceful and flowing. I come and go; I have my rhythm in this world and, even though I go far on the river, the beach is always there and the Sun is present and warming.

I leave the house and come back to my Temple, contemplating the images I have been shown. I finish my meditation quietly.

SELF-HEALING AND TRANSFORMATION

We use our intuition to perceive the structure and movement of physical and subtle energy, which is described by the intuitive function through symbolic images, words (symbolic in themselves), and feelings/sensations.

The accurate perception of our state of being is, in itself, a process that grounds and centers us, a process that brings us back to the truth of ourselves. For example, "I am neurotic, hysterical, totally unreasonable, needy and moody and impossible to be with at the moment and, knowing that to be true, I know where I am in this moment. Knowing where I am, even if it is a terrible place, is more useful than deceiving myself and trying to deceive others that I am in a good mood. Being aware that I am horrible and accepting the truth of that, here and now, allows me to find my stability and my grounding. Grounded, I am centered, and centered, I come back to my heart. In my heart, I find acceptance, and in acceptance, understanding. Accepting my neurotic, hysterical, revolting self, I find that the state passes and I become again my reasonable, balanced, neutral, loving self."

Our intuition, in its role of inner teacher (inner tuition), is always available to teach us, especially about ourselves and about who we really are. The intuition casts off illusion and veils of confusion and always reveal the truth. The truth, in itself, is a grounding thing. Once we know the truth, we know where we stand. Once we know the truth, we can situate ourselves in relation to the problem and begin to find the appropriate action/response to the problem we face. Of course, the truth is never absolute, but, with a truth that is relative to the present situation, we can already go a long way once we have that truth in our hands.

Before we can begin to heal, we must know what needs healing. We do not necessarily need to know why it needs healing, or what happened, or how things got so that healing is needed, but we do need, imperatively, to know what needs healing and where. Our intuition, with its ability to show us the actual state of how things really are, leads us very elegantly to perceive the healing need in any given situation, in any given aspect of ourselves.

When we meditate and explore the current state of being, our intuition shows us, through the richness of symbolic language, how we are, both in relation to ourselves and to our external world. With the messages we receive, we experience a simultaneous sensational and emotional reaction/response, which adds to the depth and richness of the information received.

When we receive information with which we feel at ease and with which we feel in agreement, generally speaking we can say that a healing treatment is not necessary. When information received creates a "negative" emotional reaction—uncomfortable and distressing physical symptoms, painful reactions, mental agitation, confusion, denial, and other such types of reaction—we can generally suppose that healing is necessary.

A useful guideline by which we function is the idea that, whenever something is missing, something is needed. When there is a lack, there is a need, and where there is a need, there is a place for a healing treatment.

If things are balanced, full, flowing along nicely, and there are no questions, empty spaces, intriguing obsessions, we will leave well enough alone and search elsewhere for a healing work. Of course, a good situation can always be improved upon. If we find the healing need and fulfill it, even the already good situations are going to improve, because a need fulfilled fulfills.

There are many ways to heal and many healing philosophies about how to heal, but essentially, healing is a very simple thing. We heal by loving, by loving and accepting. We heal by giving our attention to something that has been neglected. We give our loving attention to something (or someone, or a part of someone) that needs attention, because it lacks something essential to its well-being.

Something is missing and, in fulfilling the lack, in finding and filling the missing piece, reunification occurs and wholeness returns. Being healed is being returned to wholeness. Being whole is related to being integrated, and wholeness is both healthy and a state of holiness.

Learning to heal ourselves is imperative. Maintaining health is equally imperative. It is also difficult at times. The problem of self-healing can be stated like this:

> *I have a problem because I lack something. I do not know what I lack, but I know it's something, because I feel bad. I lack something and so, therefore, I need something. But what do I lack and what is my need? I don't know. I will try and find out. It's hard work alone. Finally, after much searching, I begin to recognize what I lack. But what is my need? I don't know. I will have to think about that. Finally, after much thinking, searching, and experimenting, I think I know. So how do I give it to myself? I don't know. If I knew how to give myself this need, I wouldn't have the need, and I wouldn't have the lack, because I would already have given to myself the thing that I need, before it became a problem. I don't know how to give myself what I need, because I think, in fact, it is not something I can easily give to myself. It's something someone else can give me. So I look for someone else (parents, friends, lover) to give me the thing I need, but no one seems to understand what I need. Or else they don't have time. Or else they're not interested. Or else they try to give me what I need, but what they give is not exactly what I need. So what will I do? Either I will look for someone else (therapist, teacher, healer) or I will try to give it to myself.*

Healing is the process of receiving what we need to be whole. A healer is someone who gives us what we need to be whole. The person being healed is someone who is available to receive and receives. Healing, in its true spirit, is a passage. A healer is someone who recognizes the true need of someone and gives (fulfills) the need, until such time as the person has learned how to fulfill this need for themselves. At this point, the healer is no longer necessary and the other has found what they need within themselves to bring themselves to wholeness.

Self-healing is a sacred path of personal awareness and responsibility. Sometimes it can be a lonely path. It is a path along which we learn much about our capacities and our skills, as well as our limits. There are many problems we can heal alone and there are some that are so deep and so complicated that we would be wise to recognize our limits and seek the assistance of someone else who is capable and available to guide us. Ultimately, all healing is self-healing, because healing is only possible thanks to the inner desire to be healed and whole. A healer helps us to heal ourselves. Very often, the fact of accepting our limits and asking for help accelerates the healing process to an extraordinary degree. Just as often, the presence of a loving being who takes an interest in our problem creates a healing dynamic much more powerful and effective than the dynamic created by working alone on a problem. Nonetheless, healing begins at home and home is within ourselves. Self-healing is a path of self-awareness, a path of personal empowerment, a path of growing up, and a path of great richness and wonder.

Discovering the gift of healing is akin to the discovery of love. It is a priceless gift. A divine gift. It is present in everyone who wishes to discover it. The gift of healing is an innate gift. The healing gift begins with being present and available to ourselves, with the act of paying attention to ourselves, to our deepness. Attention heals, and love and acceptance create transformation and blossoming of the inner soul.

Self-healing begins in a simple way. Even though the path may seem complicated at times, in essence, healing rests on a simple act, a simple movement. The movement of loving. In loving self, healing happens. With our intuition to guide us, to accompany us, and to teach us, we can travel the path of self-healing in trust and hope, in the expectation of positive results.

TRANSFORMATION OF SYMBOLIC IMAGES

The following meditations will give you a wealth of possibilities for taking care of your inner self and attending to the fulfillment of your deepest needs. Do not underestimate the power of these exercises. Practiced regularly, with attention to details, these meditations can and do trigger healing and transformational experiences of lasting value.

The Tree

Recommended time: 20 minutes.

- Begin with all the steps of the ritual of preparation and, when you feel ready, inform your intuitive self that you are going to do a work of self-healing using the image of the tree that your intuition has already given you.

- Ask your intuition to again give you the symbolic image of the tree. Imagine you can see this tree and its environment clearly in your mind's eye and allow yourself to imagine that you can step into the landscape of the tree with your intuitive perception. Explore the landscape, explore the tree, noting anything that has changed since the last time you were here. How do you feel?

- Imagine you have the creative freedom to change and transform this image as you like, as you feel. What needs changing? The soil? The placement of the tree? The water? The air? The Sun? What kind of attention does the tree need to be well, to be transformed, to be healed?

- Imagine you can ask the tree, "What do you need?" Allow the tree to speak to you through your telepathic channels. Let the tree explain what it needs, where and how. Imagine yourself as a psychic gardener, tending to the tree. Use your imagination. Give the tree what it needs to be well, to be healed. Change the image you began with, through your actions within it. When you feel that the tree has what it needs, stand back and observe, check your work. What has changed, what is different? How do you feel now? Be aware of the transformations you have created for your tree.

- Thank your intuitive self and, when you feel ready, end the meditation.

After the Meditation: Do a drawing of the transformed tree showing the changes compared to the original tree. You may wish to repeat this exercise several times, until the changes you have created have stabilized.

• • •

A powerful exercise you can do in relation to the tree is an adaptation of The Personal Lie and Posture (see chapter 9).

- Begin with the tree of the original meditation. Imagine you are the tree. Stand up and put yourself in the position of the tree. Take the posture and attitude of the tree.

- Explore your inner reality, the stress and tension you feel in your body, your relation to the elements of nature, your relationship to the environment around you.

- Ask yourself what you need to be well . . . Find your need and adjust your position and posture slowly and with awareness, until you find the position and the posture that you feel is appropriate for you and in which you feel well, balanced, and on the road to healing.

- Take several deep breaths, anchoring yourself in the posture you have discovered, exploring your inner state and noting the various sensations you feel in your body.

- When you feel ready, relax the posture, shake your arms and shoulders, stretch your body, and end the exercise.

• *Case Study* •

I have felt the tree needs protection, a more moderate wind and a much deeper grounding. I think a protective fence is a good idea, and some soil to protect the exposed roots. However, when I return to the tree and enter into the image to begin the work of self-healing, I no longer feel the fence is appropriate. I love the wind. I love its presence. I feel this wind like a divine wind, a guiding wind. I do not wish to protect myself from this wind. The idea of a barrier between me and the wind doesn't feel right. Instead, I imagine I open to the wind and invite the wind to blow in me, through me, rather than all around me. The wind blows in through my branches and down into the trunk, going into the Earth. The action of the wind, the direction and movement combined with the strength, helps me to ground deeper into the Earth. In accepting the presence of the wind in me, I find my grounding and I can stay stable and firm, while maintaining a deep contact with the wind, my source of inspiration. The result is stability, grounding, and the presence of inspirational guidance. I feel well with that. I can weather the storms. I am firm. I am on my hill and the wind is here with me. We are together. I am grounded.

The House

Recommended time: 20 minutes.

- Begin with the steps of the ritual of preparation and, when you feel ready, inform your intuitive self that you are going to do a work of self-healing using the symbolic image of the house that your intuition has already given you.

- Ask your intuition to present you with the image of the house again. Imagine the house and its surrounding environment clearly in your mind's eye and allow yourself to imagine that you can step into the image of the house with your intuitive perception. Explore the image, noting any changes that have occurred . . . How do you feel? Choose one of the rooms to work on, either the physical, emotional, mental, or spiritual. Which room do you feel the desire, the need, to transform? Which room needs attention most urgently? Ask your intuition to help you to make the best choice and, once you have decided, go to the room you have chosen. Imagine you have all the resources you could possibly need at your disposal, everything is possible in terms of renovations—and begin to transform the room. Do not think about what you are doing or try to interpret it, work instinctively, intuitively, transforming the room, until you have a space in which you feel well, in which you feel at home and which you feel corresponds, now, to you. Take all the time you need to settle into this transformed space. How do you feel in your body? How do you feel in your heart?

- When you feel ready, end the meditation, coming back to your everyday world.

You may wish to repeat this exercise several times until you find that the new room is well established.

• *Case Study* •

After contemplating the information I have received in the meditation, I have the desire to work on the emotional room.

I *go back to the house, and find my way to the door of the emotional room. I enter. Nothing has changed. This room represents very important things for me about the way I have been conducting my emotional life. For the past few months, I have decided to take a more disciplined attitude with my emotional self. It has worked quite well. I have much more distance. I am more calm, more self-sufficient. Also, it is wintertime, so detachment seems appropriate. But, when I see this room, I am disturbed. It's not me. It's an imposed state. A controlled room, without spontaneity, without warmth. I have succeeded too well and have gone to the opposite extreme. Also, why are the writing things there? They should be in the library, in the mental room, so that, when I am in the emotional room, it's for pleasure and joy and not the discipline and rigor of work.*

I create windows and a big glass door, a big skylight. The Sun and the light can stream into the room. I take the big serious table back to the library, as well as the writing equipment. I put a big double bed with a down quilt and lots of pillows in the room, plus a couch, chairs, a round table, flowers. I bring color and light into the space. I create a garden outside with lounge chairs and lots of sunshine. I imagine my family with me in this space, lounging around, relaxing, speaking, and simply being at home together. The cat is there, lolling about purring. I am relaxed and at home in this space now. I feel a quality of joy and pleasure in this room. I feel balanced. I have what I need. I stay a while, filling the room with my energy and enjoying the atmosphere. Then, when I feel ready, I finish the meditation and come back to my external world.

HEALING THE SUBTLE BODY

In addition to working with symbolic images to create healing, we can work directly with the subtle or energetic body, acting on the chakras and the aura with light, colors, and qualities to nourish, heal, and balance ourselves.

Meditations for the chakras can be practiced regularly and are particularly effective for balancing and recharging purposes. The three meditations proposed here are progressive in nature. The first is presented in a form that allows you to reconnect to various aspects of yourself as described through the symbolism of the chakras, using guided visualization to create reconnection, cleaning, and energizing.

In the second meditation you learn to use color as a source of healing and nourishing energy for the chakras. The third meditation teaches you how to give yourself specific qualities for healing purposes.

Chakra Meditation

Recommended time: 45 to 60 minutes.

- Close your eyes and prepare with the ritual of preparation. Breathe gently, regularly, consciously.

- When you feel ready, bring your attention to the base of your spine and the area of your lower pelvis. This is where you find your first chakra. This center of energy is related to your survival, to your physical health, to your sexuality, and to your security. Allow yourself to enter into contact with these aspects of your life and be aware of how you feel ... How do you feel in this part of your body? Do you feel relaxed here? Continue to breathe gently, maintaining your awareness in this part of your body and imagine that, as you breathe, you breathe light to this part of you, the energy of Earth, the energy of universe, mixed in your heart and flowing together through the movement of your breath, flowing like a liquid light into your first chakra. Imagine the chakra like a sphere of light, a ball of energy, and into this sphere the liquid light can flow, cleaning and filling, dissolving tension, cleaning the chakra.

- Imagine old energy, dust, and dirt, washing away down your grounding cord; the light fills your first chakra, bringing energy, strength, and fresh, clean light. Imagine your first chakra radiating light, energy, and harmony. Picture yourself in perfect health and imagine yourself secure and safe, grounded and balanced, living in ease and comfort. Imagine the feeling of being at ease with your sexuality, relaxed and at ease, your body healthy and your life secure.

- Now bring your attention to the area of your belly, to the region of your second chakra. This center of energy manages your sensuality, your moods, your emotions . . . How do you feel in this part of your body? Continue to breathe and, in breathing, bring your attention to your belly and bring light and healing energy to your second chakra, imagining light like a liquid; flowing, filling, clearing, and purifying—tension flowing out, light flowing in . . .

- Imagine your second chakra radiating light, energy, and harmony and imagine yourself at ease with the rhythm and movement of your emotional self, expressing your sensuality naturally and spontaneously, free to be yourself. Imagine yourself receiving everything you need from life, easily, without effort, in the flow . . .

- And now, bring your attention to your solar plexus, the diaphragm, the area where you find your third chakra, your center of power. From here, you act on your environment, you direct and organize, create and control . . . How do you feel in this part of your body? Continue to breathe, to stay in touch with the zone of your third chakra and, as you breathe, imagine liquid light flowing here, flowing and clearing, washing away old energy, old stories, old habits, washing away with the out breath and bringing light into your third chakra on the in breath, opening, energizing, cleaning . . . Imagine this center of energy radiating light and clarity and acknowledge within yourself your capacity to create. Imagine yourself expressing your creative power in the world, affirm within yourself your ability to finish with the past, to let go, and see yourself directing your life with confidence, creating the life that is true for you.

- Now bring your attention to your chest area, the zone of the fourth chakra. This chakra represents love and compassion, love for yourself, love for others and wisdom, the wisdom gained from the experiences of life . . . How do you feel in this part of your body? How do you feel when you breathe here? Breathe and bring light to this part of your body, liquid light, cleaning, flowing, filling your fourth chakra, letting go of old experiences, disappointments from the past, and bringing loving, liquid light here, creating space in you for love and balance. Imagine yourself giving and receiving love with ease and trust and recognize yourself as a being full of love and wisdom, a being with value, joyful and enthusiastic. Feel love flow and flower in you and know that you are loved. Be in touch with the deep reservoir of love you have in your heart to share, and let the light flow and fill you in your heart.

- Now bring your attention to your throat, to your fifth chakra. Be aware of how you feel in your throat, of how you feel about your ability to communicate in life with others. How do you feel in this part of your body? Breathe and bring light here, cleaning, clearing the fifth chakra. Allow tension to flow out, to drop away, opening the fifth chakra to receive light and healing. Imagine yourself communicating clearly, expressing your thoughts and your feelings with trust and confidence. Imagine your fifth chakra clear and radiant.

- Now bring your attention to the top of your vertebral column, inside your head, to the area of your sixth chakra, the center of energy that governs your mind, your imagination, your clairvoyance, your ability to see clearly with perspective. How do you feel about this aspect of yourself? How do you feel in this part of your body? Breathe and imagine light flowing here, opening, cleaning, and energizing . . . letting go of confusion, doubt, and hesitation, and acknowledging yourself as a seer, a visionary . . . Be thankful for your creative imagination and acknowledge your ability to create form from thought.

- Now bring your awareness to the top of your head, to the seventh chakra. This chakra governs your spiritual being, your feeling of communion with the universe, and your sense of belonging on Earth, the sense of purpose in being here, your knowingness and pure intuition. How do you feel about this part of yourself? Imagine light flowing here, cleaning and opening this center of energy, letting go of tension, of feelings of separation and solitude. Fill the seventh chakra with light and nourish your spiritual self, your divine being. See yourself acting in the world with clarity, certainty, and purpose, living the destiny of your existence with ease, with harmony, trusting life and accepting the guidance of your intuition with grace and appreciation.

- Breathe and relax, be centered and present, and bring your awareness back to your heart chakra. Be in your heart, feel the light flowing in your heart, love and light flowing in you, the stability of Earth, the light of the universe, flowing and filling you in your heart, balancing you, healing you, loving you . . .

- When you feel ready, open your eyes, feeling centered, clear, and present.

Chakras and Colors

Recommended time: 30 minutes.

- Close your eyes and prepare with the ritual of preparation. Breathe gently, regularly, consciously . . . Be aware of your connection with the Earth, with Earth energy, stabilizing and grounding you. Be aware of your connection with the energy of the universe, opening yourself to receive light from the universe all around you.

- Imagine light above your head, light from the sky, light from the source of all light, a river of light, a waterfall of light flowing to you, flowing around you, flowing within you.

- Imagine the light as the color red, a clear, strong, vibrant red, red light flowing into you, flowing into you through your seventh chakra at the top of your head and flowing down along your back, through your spine, to the first chakra.

- Imagine your first chakra as a sphere of energy, a sphere of light filling with red, liquid light, the red light flowing and filling your first chakra, nourishing your first chakra, balancing your first chakra, harmonizing your first chakra. Be aware of the sensations you feel in your pelvis as you imagine red light filling your first chakra and breathe into your lower belly, assisting the energy to circulate in this region of your body. Continue to focus internally on your first chakra, filling yourself with red light, imagining the light circulating, nourishing, balancing, and harmonizing your first chakra.

- When you feel ready, bring your attention to your second chakra and imagine that the light flowing into you becomes orange . . . orange light for the second chakra . . . yellow light for the third chakra . . . green light for the fourth chakra . . . blue light for the fifth chakra . . . purple light for the sixth chakra . . . white light for the seventh chakra . . . Taking all the time you need to fill each chakra with its corresponding color, taking all the time you need progressing through each chakra and each color at your own rhythm . . .

- When you feel ready, relax your inner concentration, open your eyes, stretch your body, and move around the room.

Chakras and Qualities

Recommended time: 30 to 45 minutes.

- Close your eyes, installing yourself comfortably, and begin with all the steps of the ritual of preparation.

- Bring your awareness to your first chakra, breathing gently into the lower belly. The quality associated with the first chakra is stability. Allow yourself to contemplate the meaning of the word "stability," thinking about what stability means to you, remembering how you feel in your body when you are stable. Contemplate stability and imagine yourself in an inner state of stability. Imagine the feeling of stability, the sensations connected to the feeling of stability. Imagine the shape of stability, images from nature that suggest stability to you. Immerse your awareness as fully as you can in the atmosphere of stability, and imagine your first chakra absorbing the quality

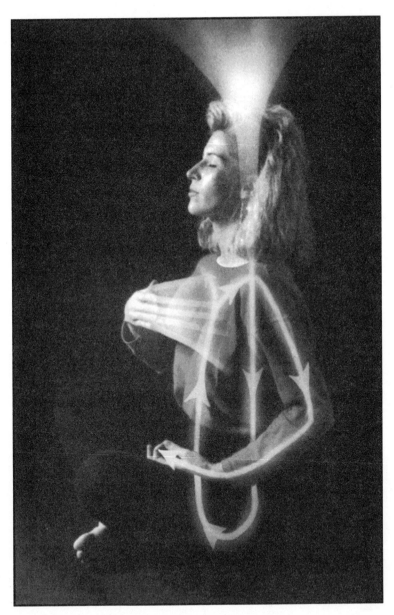

Figure 13. Sending healing light to self: to the heart.

of stability, in the same way you have imagined the chakra absorbing light and color. Maintain awareness of your first chakra for some minutes, creating within yourself, with your imagination and your memory, the inner atmosphere of stability. Ask the light to become the quality of stability and imagine the quality of stability as a healing force, bringing you what you need for the well-being of your first chakra. Imagine yourself radiating the quality of stability, and expressing stability through your actions in the world.

• When you feel ready, bring your attention to your second chakra, breathing into your belly, being aware of this part of yourself. The quality associated with the second chakra is spontaneity. Contemplate the meaning that spontaneity has for you . . . and continue the meditation, as for the first chakra, taking your time with each chakra, with each quality, progressing through the meditation at your rhythm.

• The quality associated with the third chakra is power.

• The quality associated with the fourth chakra is joy.

• The quality associated with the fifth chakra is authenticity.

• The quality associated with the sixth chakra is certainty.

• The quality associated with the seventh chakra is communion.

• When you feel ready to end the meditation, take several deep, full breaths and open your eyes, noting how you feel in your body, how you feel in your spirit.

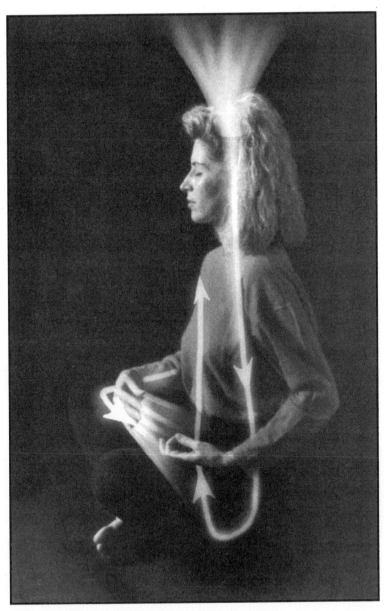

Figure 14. Sending healing light to self: to the belly.

THE AURA

It is important, in a work of personal evolution, that we have a clear sense of ourselves in relation to our external world. To know who we are, we must be able to differentiate between ourselves and others. This may seem a rather obvious statement, but, in reality, it is often difficult to discern clearly the limits of "self" in relation to "other." In an absolute sense, we can argue that separation does not exist at all. Everything is connected, the universe is one being and we are all cells of this vast being, intrinsically interrelated with each other.

Working with energy, we learn to extend our awareness, to penetrate and "merge" with matter. In healing practice, we learn to enter into the reality of another, to "feel" the other, in order to perceive the lacks and needs for healing purposes. It is for exactly this reason that we must also work to establish and define our personal energetic limits. If I know who I am, "where I begin and end," I can expand my consciousness into the reality of another in security, because, knowing who I am, I can go toward the other without losing myself and I can come back when the exercise is finished.

Knowing how to enter into rapport with someone else is a tremendously useful skill. We do this unconsciously each time we put ourselves "in the place" of someone else. Learning how to manage this skill consciously is a work of great personal awareness. Learning to merge and separate energetically for purposes of intuitive perception and healing is a work that requires great skill and lots of practice.

In exercises of self-healing, we create what is called a personal boundary as a means of self-protection. We protect ourselves from the external world, not because the world is a nasty, horrible, menacing place out to harm us, but because we are delicate and sensitive and need protection from the chaos of the external world so we can stay more easily centered and balanced within ourselves. The external world is often perturbing, and other people are full of their own problems and inner chaotic processes of evolution and transformation.

With awareness of our own personal boundaries, we gain an understanding of the difference between our energy, our "atmosphere," and the atmosphere of others. We learn to discern with more lucidity the difference between "our stuff" and "the stuff" of others, thus gaining invaluable insights into the process of projection in relationships.

The personal boundary helps us to stay centered in our axis and to stay focused in our own personal rhythm, our own movement. Protected from dispersion, we stop wasting our energy and can stay focused on the path of the moment.

Creating and Maintaining Personal Boundaries

Recommended time: 20 minutes.

- Begin with the ritual of preparation.

- Bring your attention to the limits of your physical body and feel the contact of your clothes against your skin, the sensation of the air touching you . . .

- Imagine the seven chakras, radiating energy from the axis of your body and overflowing all around you, creating your personal energy field, your personal aura.

- Become aware of the places around your body where you feel vulnerable, exposed . . . and the places where you feel secure and protected.

- Imagine your aura as a field of light, a field of energy, like a woven tapestry of light, with some areas thicker, some areas thinner, some worn out, and others . . .

- Imagine you can repair your aura intuitively, pulling out energy that doesn't belong to you, cleaning your aura of old energies. Then mend your aura, filling in the places that are too empty, protecting areas where you feel vulnerable, smoothing out your aura, until it is the shape of an eggshell, smooth and balanced, all around you.

- Imagine your boundary a comfortable distance from your body, with all the holes mended, everything balanced, and you, centered and balanced, inside.

Do this meditation regularly, checking places of weakness and reinforcing them until they stay strong. This exercise is particularly useful before and after stressful experiences, conflicts, and confrontions.

FOLLOWING YOUR PATH

Using our intuition to explore choices available to us creates a situation where the spiritual direction of our life is always taken into consideration before a decision is reached that affects the path of our daily life. Intuition, in its roles of inner guide, teacher, and soul-gathering experience, will not necessarily indicate the easiest or most comfortable direction. However, we can count on the intuition to guide us toward choices that create inner growth, evolution, and the expression of our essential personal qualities. It is important to remember that, for the soul, experience is the purpose of life. From experience comes wisdom and from wisdom, acceptance and detachment. Liberation from attachment creates the freedom to be authentic and, in the atmosphere of authenticity, the soul is free to live fully and gather a full quota of earthly experience. Every soul has its individual purpose, but, globally speaking, the greatest challenge for every incarnated soul is the challenge of self-realization. We realize the truth of who we are thanks to the tasks and missions we undertake during our lives. It is often the more difficult experiences that cause us to grow the most and for which we can be the most grateful in retrospect.

Essentially, we are free souls, free to choose and create the direction of our activities as we wish. Even in karmic obligations and debts, we have a choice. For every choice we make, there is a consequence. Even though we are essentially free, every soul has a path to follow. The path is not a physical path, requiring us to be in a certain place at a certain time, but is rather a fluid, flowing directional path of experience. As a soul, I incarnate with a purpose. To fulfill this purpose, I have many possibilities. It is not so much what I do, when and with whom, but more how I do things and with what level of awareness that causes my evolution and thus the accomplishment of my purpose.

My soul, in its ultimate wisdom, knows the experiences it needs to evolve according to its destiny. Parents and family are chosen based on the fundamental life experiences needed by the soul for its evolution. For this reason, many old souls are born into quite difficult family situations. Lessons are learned young and experiences are gained quickly, enabling the soul to progress more rapidly through life to achieve the purpose of the incarnation while still young enough to accomplish and integrate the purpose.

When we align ourselves with our intuitive self, we align ourselves with our soul and spirit, thus realigning with our essential spiritual purpose. The spiritual purpose naturally expresses itself through the realization of a path, or way of being. This way of being has a philosophical aspect, as well as a means of practical application. As spiritual beings, we realize who we are, thanks to the journey along the path. The path is a means through which we arrive at the end. In the paradox of spiritual initiation and mastery, we never actually arrive anywhere, even though we are eternally in the process of going somewhere with the purpose of arriving. The path is a means, giving us a direction and a sense of purpose, but it is the awareness we bring to the journey as we travel that results in evolution of the soul and the gaining of wisdom through the integration of the experiences lived.

When we find our path and live in accordance with it, life takes on a different quality, a different atmosphere. Realigned with our deepness and connected to a sense of personal and spiritual purpose, a quality of trust begins to install itself in us. Trusting ourselves, trusting the universe, we can relax the control and begin to let things flow. Trusting in the path, trusting in the flow, we stay more easily centered on the path, allowing the flow to guide us and support us along the way. Realigned with the sense of our verticality (axis heaven/Earth), we gradually lose our attachment to the way we think things and people should be and we open ourselves to the experience of how things and people actually are. Liberating ourselves to be ourselves, we discover our external reality as a movement much more fluid and supple than we had previously imagined. By liberating ourselves, others too begin to feel liberated in our presence and can more easily be themselves. Thus life takes on a new dimension, a dimension of suppleness, of possibilities, and of renewed hope, as we realize that healing is possible and transformation inevitable.

Our intuition guides us to choose the way of evolution. Evolution is a process of change, transformation, and healing, of personal mastery and self-realization. Our intuition will never guide us toward a path that is not ultimately in our best interests. The path may not be easy. The path may reveal our weaknesses to ourselves and others and demand much personal effort, but the reward will far outweigh the efforts we are invited to make.

As we align ourselves more and more with our true purpose and our true being, as we trust more and more this new way of functioning, we allow the movement to guide us and show us the way. We go willingly, no longer doubting and hesitating as we go. We feel the stability of the Earth and the luminous presence of the universe accompanying us and we find our balance, our axis, and our place in the movement of life flowing through us.

Existence is loving, generous, and spontaneous. Open to the possibility of friendly horizons, the path becomes a pleasure. No longer an arduous task of impossible responsibilities, life reveals itself as a creative playground of self-expression and personal realization.

The three following meditations will help you to make sense of your personal world, your current experiences, and the reasons why you are in relationship with the people close to you in your daily life. With these techniques of intuitive practice, you can situate yourself more rapidly and more clearly in relation to people around you, no longer wasting time unnecessarily worrying and analyzing the psychological position and behaviors of yourself and others. Going beyond the psychological framework of perception, you can perceive yourself and others as beings evolving, beings with a movement, beings with something to share and exchange. At times, the exchange is experienced as a flowing movement and at times it seems in conflict. Going beyond the experience of conflict to rediscover the harmonious flow of true exchange is a liberating experience for everyone involved.

Decision-Making

For exploring possible pathways and understanding the advantages and inconveniences of each possibility, making a choice that is in alignment with the path of the soul.

Recommended time: 20 to 40 minutes.

- Follow all the steps of the ritual of preparation and, when you feel ready, bring your awareness to the decision you are facing. Be in contact with how you feel at this moment and be in acceptance of the various emotions you may be experiencing in relation to the choices you are exploring. Let go of stress and tension, let go of worry and fear and breathe into your belly, grounding yourself and relaxing. Be aware of the fact that, in relation to the choice you are facing, there are several possibilities available to you and affirm within yourself that you are now going to explore these possibilities from an intuitive perspective.

- Imagine yourself strolling in the garden of your Temple and, as you stroll, you reflect on the problem you are facing, simply allowing thoughts and feelings to come and go . . . Within yourself, define all possible options open to you . . . for example, with a job offer, either you can take the job or not.

- Imagine, as you walk in your garden, that you find yourself on a path and, on the path, you arrive at a crossroad, where the path divides and becomes 2, 3, 4 . . . paths.

- Imagine the first path as the path of one option, the second path as the path of another option . . . and give each path a name, a title. Be aware of how you feel in your body and begin to walk along the first path, the path of the first option, and note very carefully the path itself, the landscape, the atmosphere, the weather, and, above all, the way you feel within yourself as you take this path. Where is this path going? What is your destination? What will this option give you? Are there other people on the path? What inner qualities does this path demand of you? What inner qualities do you need to succeed on this path? Is it a path that feels right for you? Be open to the impressions you receive, to the physical sensations you experience in your body and to your feeling in the heart. Imagine as you journey along this path that you come across an old wise being who is waiting for you. Create a contact with this being and allow yourself to ask advice from him or her about this path . . . about what it can give you, what it can teach you.

- When you feel satisfied, go back along the path, arriving at the crossroad where you began and repeat the same procedure along the path that represents option number two.

- Repeat the same procedure with each possible option, until you have intuitively explored all the options possible for the choice you are facing.

- When you have finished exploring, return to your Temple, install yourself well into your centered intuitive mode and ask yourself: "Which of these paths corresponds to the path of my soul, to my true and correct path?" Be available for the response you receive. Ask yourself: "Which of these paths brings joy to my heart?" Be available for the response you receive. When you feel ready, relax your awareness and return to your normal state of consciousness.

Difficult Situations

For understanding, accepting, and opening the way for transformation of difficult situations, where the lesson and purpose of the situation is not evident and you have a desire that the situation be resolved.

Recommended time: 30 minutes.

- After preparing yourself with the steps necessary to enter into intuitive mode, affirm within yourself that you are going to explore the situation in question with the help of your intuitive self, using the technique of symbolic images to bring you insights and understanding.

- Imagine you are walking in your Temple garden and, as you walk, contemplate the situation and the difficulties you are experiencing in relation to the situation.

- Imagine the other people, if there are any, who are involved in the situation with you and feel within your deepness your desire to be liberated from the difficulties of this problem. Feel your desire to be free to continue on your path in harmony and imagine the path of your life as a path stretching out in front of you. As you walk on the path, you see ahead of you an obstacle blocking the path, an obstacle in front of you which causes you to slow down, to stop. Regard the obstacle blocking the path and be aware of what it is, of the form it takes, of its size, its substance, and its atmosphere . . . What is your immediate, instinctive reaction in the face of the obstacle? What emotion do you feel? How do you imagine the obstacle got here on your path? Is it a natural obstacle or man-made? Which part of the obstacle "belongs" to you and which part to the other people involved in the situation? What does the obstacle tell you? Most importantly, by stopping on your path to deal with this obstacle, what are you being taught? What do you have to understand? If, instead of struggling against this obstacle, you accept it, what happens? What are the inner resources, the inner qualities you need to overcome the obstacle, to go beyond it? Ask your intuition to help you to discover these qualities inside yourself, and to show you the way to go beyond the obstacle you are facing. Once beyond it, look back and observe the obstacle from your new position and larger perspective. How do you see it now?

- Remember the qualities you needed to overcome the obstacle. When you feel ready, recenter yourself in your Temple and then, taking several deep breaths, relax your intuitive focus and open your eyes.

- The qualities you need to overcome the obstacle in your meditation are the same qualities you need in the situation you are facing in your real life.

- Return to your inner state of intuitive awareness and imagine the situation as it is happening in your actual life. See yourself managing the situation with the qualities you need, finding your way with these qualities, going beyond the difficulties of the situation. Stay connected to the desire of your heart to resolve the situation so you can learn, integrate, and move on to other things.

Relationships

For conflict resolution, clarification of the purpose of the relationship, and for creating an atmosphere where a quality of harmony and communion is possible in the relationship.

Recommended time: 30 minutes.

- After following the steps of preparation, inform your intuitive self that you wish to explore your world of personal relationships with the help of your intuition.

- Imagine the person with whom you are experiencing difficulties and contemplate, for a few minutes, the nature of the difficulties you are experiencing. Imagine this person comes to your Temple and enters inside the sacred space of your Temple, coming toward you to visit and speak with you.

- Imagine the person is available to listen to you, and you to him or her. Speak from the truth of yourself, explaining to the person the problems you have and the way you feel, and imagine the response of the person to the things you have said, imagine that the other speaks his or her truth to you in relation to the problem. When you have finished expressing the problem, say to the person how you would like to live in the relationship, how you would like it to be between you. Send to the other the image and the feeling of your preferred way of being together in the relationship. Ask your intuition to show you and/or tell you the true purpose of your relationship with this person.

- Ask the following questions of your intuitive self: "What do I have to teach this person?" "What do I have to learn from this person?" "What does the other have to teach me?" "Do we still have things to teach each other?" "What do I need to let go of (ideas, stories, judgments), so that this relationship can evolve and prosper?" "What do I need to accept in the other?" Be available for the responses you receive and be aware of how you feel in your body as you progress with the meditation. At the end, reconfirm your heart-connection to the person and imagine the person leaving your Temple. When you feel ready, end the meditation.

Pay attention the next time you see the person to how things feel and/or are different than before you did this meditation.

HEALING YOUR WORLD

Anger, resentment, and bitterness are emotional states that block the function of love in life and therefore limit the circulation of energy in the heart chakra. There is no question that human relationships are complex, often paradoxical, and certainly full of contradictions. We are often deceived, disappointed, and disillusioned by the so-called "imperfections" of the people to whom we are the closest. Conflict, though terribly uncomfortable to live through, forms an intrinsic part of most deep and meaningful relationships. It would be nice to live in eternal harmony, but here on Earth, harmony is a much appreciated and rather rare state of experience. If we are authentic and committed to the path of self-realization, it is virtually impossible to go through life without bothering someone, at some time. If we live close to someone else who follows the same path of authenticity, they are sure to behave (from time to time, if not more often), in a manner that evokes a conflicted reaction from us. At times, conflict has nothing to do with the question of authenticity.

We can feel betrayed, ripped off, or tricked by another person. We can experience something with the other that causes us to reach the decision to terminate the relationship. We can become so angry that it is simply no longer possible to communicate with the other, so we cut off the relationship.

It is quite seldom that a relationship ends quietly and in peace, both parties calm, clear, and in the heart. A relationship of this quality is not a relationship we would feel the desire to terminate!

We have all ended relationships. Life is a process of meeting and parting. Just think for a moment of all the people you have known in your life, with whom you no longer have any contact. For most of these people, the parting was easy, natural, in harmony with the natural flow of things for both of you. But there are always some relationships that end in conflict, with unfinished business, with resentment, anger, and bitterness.

In fact, these relationships are not finished at all, even though we may never see or speak to the person involved. Relationships of this nature drain our energy. We are energetically imprisoned by the unfinished business of the relationship. We are not free and neither is the other. These unfinished conflicts preoccupy us on an unconscious level and create an energetic situation where our energy and attention is not available for living what is happening in present time, in our current life. We cannot commit ourselves to the present moment because of our preoccupation with the past. To be truly free in the present, we are obliged to cut our links to the past. Breaking with the past does not mean disassociating ourselves from the past or from our memories of the past. It simply means "liberating" charged memories, so the energy can be used in present time.

Acceptance and forgiveness are two qualities essential to the path of healing. To create a better world, we are obliged to heal the world we are in. There is no other way. There is no other world. The inner world of our heart is broken and scarred from many battles, and wisdom gained is often gained with great sadness and disillusionment. We are often right, but just as often, the other is right. And as often as we are right, we are wrong.

Psychological warfare exhausts the heart and wearies the soul. Moreover, it builds barriers around the heart that become virtually impenetrable over time. Hate, resentment, and judgment are strong emotions, poison for the heart. Acceptance brings healing to the heart and soul, and forgiveness allows us to go beyond the problem, free to engage ourselves in new adventures of the heart.

To accept somebody else does not necessarily mean to agree with them or to obey them. To accept a situation does not mean giving your approval to the situation. It simply means accepting. Not fighting against. Not being opposed to. Acceptance is an inner state, a state of inner letting go, where we renounce the need to be right, to know best, to be superior. In acceptance, we surrender to the situation as it is, accepting it as it is, even if it is not how we would like, or how we think it should be. We accept the other as they are. We accept ourselves as we are. We accept the imperfections, the contradictions, and the paradoxes, and we let go of the struggle of our desire that it be otherwise.

Acceptance is not the same as forgiveness. Acceptance allows us to let go of our attachment to the idea that the situation or the person be other than it, he, or she is. Forgiveness allows us to let go totally of the situation or the person. Forgiveness finishes things. Forgiveness is like a death, and from death rebirth is possible.

Sometimes we would like to accept and forgive, but we cannot because we are not yet ready. Righteous indignation has its place in the world of emotional expression, as does anger, resentment, and loss of respect. When we have experienced a strong conflict within ourselves or with another, we must also respect the truth of what we are in the process of experiencing. To pretend to accept while experiencing emotions of rejection and resentment is hypocritical and totally unauthentic. Better to express the truth of anger than to pretend to be charitable. If we accept the emotions we experience, we give them the possibility to transform into other states of experience.

Acceptance begins always with ourselves. If we are not ready to accept, it is better to be honest and aware. Knowing where we are, we are always in a safe and true place.

Acceptance and Forgiveness Meditation

Recommended time: 20 to 30 minutes.

- Breathe, center, and bring yourself into your heart. Be present with yourself, and available for this exercise of healing.

- Imagine someone with whom you have had a problem and, because of this problem, you suffer in your heart. Call the person and imagine he or she comes into your Temple and sits down, facing you. Stay in your heart and express to this person the things you need to say . . . "What I need to say to you, that I couldn't/wouldn't is . . ." and unload your heart of all the unsaid things.

- Imagine the other, open and available to listen to you, simply listening, accepting what you say. Feel your heart opening, letting go . . . Allow the emotion, the feeling, to flow. When you feel ready, say to the other, "I accept you as you are," or "Please accept me as I am," or "I accept myself as I am."

- Be in the atmosphere of acceptance and be aware of how it feels to accept in your heart. If you wish to explore forgiveness, imagine yourself in front of the other and say "I forgive you," or "I forgive myself," or ask for forgiveness: "Please forgive me." Feel the atmosphere of forgiveness and allow this quality of energy to open your heart, to clean your heart, and heal the wounds of the past, freeing you to breathe and to feel the deepness of your heart, open, available to live and to love.

Repeat this meditation for as many people as needed, as often as you like. This meditation can also be done as a letter-writing exercise.

MANIFESTING TECHNIQUES—
CREATING YOUR PATH

Every thought we think has a consequence in our lives. Every thought creates a result. The fact that we do not always immediately perceive the result does not mean that the result is not in the process of being created. A result is not always created in a form existing outside ourselves. The result of a thought has its repercussions within us, before we can experience the external consequences. The more awareness we have of our thoughts and the atmosphere of our inner world, the more we can determine the relationship we create in our external world. The external world is a mirror of our internal state and our perceptions of reality are almost always influenced by the atmosphere of our inner world of thoughts and feelings.

We have only to regard the actual life we live, the life of home, work, and family, to receive clear feedback about the quality of our belief systems and, more importantly, our beliefs about ourselves. Our lives are a clear reflection of who we believe ourselves to be. Every single thing and person existing in our lives is there because we created them. We are all magicians and manifesters, essentially creative. Unfortunately, we have difficulty accepting responsibility for this fact, so the capacity is often only mildly developed and even more sporadically managed.

The work of manifesting essentially demands that we accept responsibility for the creation and management of our lives. It is a work requiring awareness, vigilance, and inner discipline, a work of mental training, a work of personal empowerment.

With the applied techniques of manifestation, we learn that the more we are aware of our thoughts, the more we can choose and create the quality of our lives. Awareness is the key to the transformation of belief systems. With awareness we have choice, and choice is implicit in the concept of freedom and ultimate liberty. We can choose our lives and we can create the life of our choice. With willpower and determination, a life can be forged and built according to our desires and we can be proud of the results of all our efforts.

The dimension of intuition allows us to clarify with precision the quality of life we desire, as well as the various concrete components of that life. Rather than forging ahead and exhausting ourselves in a struggle against the elements to create the life we want, we adopt an attitude of availability and awareness within ourselves and we allow the natural movement of life to create itself into the form and structure that corresponds to our deepest needs and desires. Within ourselves, we hold the vision of the life we would like and, staying in contact with our intuition and the relationship we have with the vertical, we allow the flow of life to organize us, and it, into the appropriate functioning pattern. Clear within ourselves about our preferences, we can say no to the conditions that do not correspond to our vision and yes to those criteria that do.

In order to succeed with the techniques of manifestation it is above all essential that you believe within yourself that you deserve to receive. Manifesting is, on one hand, a work of creating, but, more than that, it is a movement of receiving. If you believe that you deserve to receive, life will be able to give to you and you will be able to accept the gifts given.

The steps of manifesting must be followed precisely and progressively to achieve the desired result.

1. *Be aware of the actual situation.* In other words, know where you are and how you feel about the situation you would like to modify and/or transform.

2. *Accept the situation as it is in present time.* It may not be how you want it to be, but it is how it is, so accept it. Acceptance helps you to be in present time and present time is the moment of creative power.

3. *Choose what you want.* Be clear about your preference and be precise about the changes you would like.

4. *Imagine having it now.* Bring it into present time in your imagination, even if it does not actually exist concretely in present time yet. Begin to live with the attitude that you have it now.

Creating Your Life

1. *Write a list* of all the things you like and you do not like in your life. This list can be as personal or as general as you like.

As you write this list, think about your life and about the quality of your life, being aware of how you feel generally and precisely about the life you have; work, family, friends, interests, etc.

2. *Read your list* out loud to yourself and find within yourself an attitude of acceptance toward yourself and your life as it is now.

3. *Imagine you can create* the life of your dreams, of your heart's desire. What would be the perfect life for you? Imagine. Where do you live? With whom? Doing what? How often?

Imagine you are one year in the future and, during this last year, your life has reorganized itself to become the life of your dreams. Describe the life of your dreams as though you are living it now in present time, writing down all the relevant details, all the important points. Ask yourself the following questions: Is it possible (to have, to do, to be, to experience)? Is it worth having? Will it give me what I really want? Am I ready to do what is necessary to have it? You must be able to answer YES to all these questions.

4. *Imagine having it now.* Close your eyes and allow yourself to picture your ideal life, the life you have described on paper. Imagine your ideal life in as much detail as possible. See yourself engaged in

the activities of life with the people you wish to spend your time with, at work, at home, etc. Remember the words of your Eternal Key and repeat them within yourself, imagining you are radiating the atmosphere of your Eternal Key. Be aware of how you feel in your body, and of how you feel as you imagine your ideal life. Within yourself, you can affirm: "This is for me."

When you feel ready, open your eyes.

Treasure Map

Take a large sheet of cardboard, scissors, glue, colored pencils, felt tip pens, plus several old magazines that have photographs and advertising inside. Search through these magazines until you find images that correspond to the life of your dreams. You may find photos of houses, landscapes, people. You may find words and sentences you like, written for advertising purposes. Cut out these words and pictures and arrange them artistically on the cardboard, pasting them to create a collage. Represent yourself within the collage and write your Eternal Key somewhere on the page. Using colors, images, and your creative inspiration, create a collage that symbolically represents your ideal life. While you are creating the treasure map, think about what you are doing and be in touch with your desire to transform your life, so that you can live a life that corresponds to your deep desires and wishes.

Do not become preoccupied with questions about how you should implement the changes. Simply stay in contact with your wish that your life transform itself to become the life of your dreams. Feel within yourself your willingness and availability to receive this gift.

When your treasure map is finished, place it somewhere where you see it regularly and, every time you see it, think about what it means to you. Take the time to appreciate the colors, the images, and the fact that it is you who created it.

Figure 15. Treasure map: technique for manifestation.

Figure 16. Treasure map: technique for manifestation.

Pink-Bubble Meditation

- Follow all the steps of the ritual of preparation and when you feel ready, imagine in front of you, at eye level, a large pink bubble.

- Imagine you can see yourself inside the bubble, living the ideal life you have imagined for yourself. The pink bubble is full of the images of you and your life and it is full of the atmosphere of the life you have chosen to give yourself.

- Imagine that the bubble descends and enters into your axis at the level of your first chakra. Visualize the bubble floating gently, arriving in your first chakra, and affirm within yourself: "I give form to my vision." Imagine the bubble rising gently, arriving in your second chakra, and affirm: "I give feeling to my vision." The bubble rises, arriving in your third chakra, and you affirm: "I give power and action to my vision." The bubble rises, floating into your fourth chakra and you affirm: "I give love and wisdom to my vision." The bubble rises to your fifth chakra and you affirm: "I give words and understanding to my vision." The bubble rises to your sixth chakra and you affirm: "I give clarity and perspective to my vision." The bubble rises to your seventh chakra and you affirm: "I give harmony to my vision," and "I bless my vision with light and the sense of purpose."

• Imagine the bubble floating up over your head, floating out into the sky, full of your energy, of your atmosphere, and of the qualities you have given it. Imagine the bubble full of you and your vision . . . the bubble floats into the sky and far away, high up, it bursts into hundreds of fragments and the wind carries the fragments away into the four directions. Each fragment contains your energy . . . let it go, watch the fragments disperse with the wind, and know that life will bring your wish to you. The energy you have sent out will come back to you. It is simply a question of time.

The Song of the Heart

• Breathe, ground and center yourself. Bring your awareness to your chest area and breathe fully and deeply, becoming more and more present in your heart, more and more available to yourself, to your deepness, to your truth.

• In the sanctuary of your heart, in the stillness of your Temple, look into your heart, and see the desires of your heart, the needs of your heart. Allow yourself to feel what you need to be well in your heart . . . What would bring joy to your heart? If you could create for yourself anything at all, what would it be? Feel what is true for you, and choose, choose what you would like to live, to receive, to give, to have, to be . . .

- Within your mind's eye, create a clear image of yourself receiving and living your heart's desire. See it and feel it as though it exists in this moment for you . . . you have it, you touch it, you hear it, you smell it, you see it, you appreciate it . . .

- Imagine yourself managing it and maintaining it, accepting responsibility for your creation. Allow yourself to feel the quality of gratitude, thankfulness, and thank yourself and existence for this possibility to bring joy to your heart, to bring joy to your soul.

- Imagine yourself singing, singing with joy, with pleasure . . . receiving the blessing of your heart's desire, staying centered in the feeling of receiving, of receiving the things that bring joy to your heart, centered in the feeling of the song that springs from your heart, the song of thanks, of blessing, and of hope.

- Stay present, breathing, allowing this feeling to spread all through your body . . . when you feel ready, open your eyes, stretch your body, and relax your attention.

5

UTILIZING YOUR
INTUITION
WITH OTHERS

CHAPTER FIFTEEN

Being Clear

We know that intuition functions as a means through which we can perceive the true nature of reality existing within and around us. Our capacity to perceive clearly is dependent on many factors—the depth and stability of our trance state, the subject we are perceiving, personal preconceived ideas and conditioning, and our inner state. Because of the fact that our intuition functions through us, i.e., through the sense mechanisms of our body/being (seeing, hearing, feeling, smelling, tasting), the perceptions we receive are always intrinsically linked to the relationship we have with ourselves on an essential level.

The intuition serves as a mirror, reflecting back to us our strengths and weaknesses, as well as our inner relationship with ourselves and the functioning of our physical bodies and five senses. If, in life, we have difficulty expressing ourselves with words, we will experience the same difficulty with the function of the intuition. If we suffer from a lack of imagination, it will probably be difficult in the intuition exercises to receive images. On a more physical level, we find that someone who is out of touch with their own body and the world of sensation, will naturally experience the same difficulties "feeling" with their intuitive senses.

It seems to be a universal law that the level at which we perceive the deepness and truth of another will be the same as the level at which we perceive the deepness and truth of ourselves. In other words, if we cannot see ourselves clearly, if we cannot discern our own emotional state or understand ourselves, it is silly to assume that we will succeed in doing so with somebody else. So it is essential to engage in personal transformational work on ourselves in order to deeply and fully develop the intuition. Just as important is the necessity to work more deeply on those aspects of ourselves that we experience as blocked or disassociated, and at the same time to develop the capacities with which we are more at ease. The utilization of our well-developed natural abilities will help to maintain enthusiasm and high self-esteem during those periods when we face and resolve the problem areas of our intuitive function.

We have discovered through intuition research and training programs that working on ourselves helps us to work on others, and working on others provides us with the occasion to continue to work on ourselves. The process of exchange, of two people practicing on each other, is the ideal environment for personal growth and accelerated learning. Even though it is essential to utilize the techniques of intuition development on ourselves, it can be somewhat difficult to sort through the information we receive and to distinguish what is intuition, what is conjecture, what is fantasy, and what is real. Working on another, we naturally have more distance and can stay more neutral, because we have less personal involvement. An intuitive session with a stranger is infinitely more simple than the same session practiced with a family member. When we know absolutely nothing about somebody, we can be sure that the information we receive is being received intuitively.

Our own personal internal world is literally a world unto itself. If we can learn to be objective, neutral, compassionate, and centered with regards to ourselves, then we will be able to utilize these qualities later on when we begin to practice on others.

It is normal, in the beginning of intuition practice, to make mistakes. In the process of clearing ourselves, we may pass through phases of projection, power, and manipulation. We will give interpretations to the symbols we perceive and, later, may realize that these interpretations were not exactly accurate or appropriate. We must simply be conscious of the possibility of making mistakes, remembering the wisdom contained in the saying, "If you are not willing to make mistakes, you will never make anything."

Through mistakes, we learn, and what we learn becomes integrated as a wealth of personal experience. In our quest for personal lucidity and excellence, it is, however, preferable not to repeat the same mistakes. Constant repetition of mistakes is a sign of unconsciousness and personal delusion, reminding us of the necessity to pay attention, learn, and progress beyond our habitual patterns of behavior.

CHAPTER SIXTEEN

Rules of Practice

Intuition is a sacred capacity, sacred because it is the expression of our divine aspect acting through the physical world, and sacred also because of its tremendous power to transform physical matter, mind, and spirit.

With our intuition, we experience our ability to feel, see, and hear the truth. In other words, we experience our capacity to separate illusion from truth and to perceive the truth of a situation, an event, ourselves, or another person, relative to the movement of existence in any given moment. When we exercise our intuition on somebody else, we place ourselves in a position of enormous responsibility in relation to the other. We assume, in these moments, one of several archetypal roles—healer, teacher, guide, priest, priestess, god, goddess—and each of these roles demands a tremendous personal clarity and ethical integrity on our part.

We are obliged to accept responsibility for the position of power we assume, so that we can conduct the session with authority and certainty. We must never abuse the power with which we have been entrusted by violating, in one way or another, the integrity of the person with whom we are working. We must always remember, when we practice using our intuitive skills on others, that our primary objective is to assist in the transformational and evolutionary process of the other and, from a transpersonal perspective, to assist in the evolution of humanity. In these roles, we act as a bridge, a link, between light and matter, offering our services to light so that she may marry with matter and bring our world back to light. Rendering service, we too are healed and transformed. Assuming the role of teacher, healer, guide, priestess—and assuming it well—can bring us much personal fulfillment, recognition, gratitude, and eventually even financial gain, if we engage ourselves in the intuitive work on a professional level.

The places of healer, spiritual teacher, and psychic reader are unusual roles to assume in today's world. Once we find ourselves relegated to a role in which we have authority, we are immediately faced with the challenge of managing, with wisdom, the power given that accompanies the roles. The ego, being the self-centered, delusion-oriented, power maniac that it is, can easily fall into myriad traps once it experiences the position of authority and unlimited creative power provided through the dynamic of a "practitioner/client" relationship. Because of the danger of the ego and its propensity toward self-aggrandizement, territorial acquisition, and power games of domination and conquest, personal spiritual transformational work is essential, especially if we are to assume, with integrity and sound ethics, the role of teacher/healer within the society.

Most talented teachers and healers are conscious of and try to manage as best they can, the considerable power of their egos. The ego needs to be perceived as an aspect of ourselves requiring management and limits, rather than as a demon needing to be demolished. Thanks to our egos, to our sense of ourselves as personalities we have something to say, ideas to share, philosophies to debate, teachings to transmit. It is, in part, thanks to the ego that we even dare to propose intuitive readings and healings to others. The great trap of the ego lies in its sense of solitary existence, the tendency to think that it, and it alone, is responsible for its success, greatness, cleverness, etc. Intuition is not ego. Intuition is soul. Soul knows that it belongs ultimately to the vastness of the source, to the dancing light, to the god heart of the universe. Intuition knows that the concept of individuality is a construction of the mind/ego that differentiates it from the Great Oneness in order to achieve a certain task during a particular incarnation.

Intuition knows that we are all ultimately and deeply one being, a collective consciousness, one soul. Therefore, to harm somebody else is to harm oneself, and to heal somebody else is to heal oneself. If, when we assume the role of healer, we can always remember this truth, then our ego will stay in its appropriate framework and the interventions we practice will be just and appropriate for the persons on whom we act.

When we work on another, it is imperative that we view the other as a being of intelligence and integrity. We perceive others as beings containing within themselves all the resources they need to realize their purpose and their destiny. One aspect of our role is to assist others to access these inner resources and qualities, always encouraging them to look, first and foremost, to themselves for answers and healing. The others in front of us are, like ourselves, beings born from a sacred place, beings in the process of realizing, of remembering, who they are in the truth of themselves. Like ourselves, these beings need love, acceptance, and respect to help them to find themselves. By creating an atmosphere of respect and integrity, and by conducting our work with impeccable ethical standards, we create a sacred ambiance in which transformation and healing are a natural outcome.

When we open ourselves to our intuition, we open ourselves to our truth and to the living intelligence of the universe. We place our trust in this intelligence and allow it to speak and act through us, at the same time "directing" its interaction through our conscious awareness. Through our intention, the intelligent energy acts at one or another level of consciousness. For this reason, we must always remember to channel the energy with the intention that it act for the highest possible good of all beings involved in the intervention taking place. Praying for the highest possible good aligns us with light, creation, and evolution and naturally protects us from the traps of personal interest and manipulation into which it can be so easy to fall on an unconscious level. When we align with the intention of acting for the highest good, the universe lends us its energy and light, empowering us to a greater degree than when we act alone. In concert with the universe and acting with light as our guide, we are capable of doing a great work, a healing work of depth, precision, and truth. Once we have experienced the tremendous blessing of working in collaboration with light, once we have experienced firsthand the sense of communion resulting from this collaboration, we lose all interest in working "alone." Knowing that, in truth, we are one with light, we become totally committed to the path of light and, through this path, we work to bring others to the realization of the same truth. From this perspective, the use of our intuitive and healing gifts becomes a service rendered for the highest good of all beings, including ourselves, those we work on, and others. Our work becomes an integral part of our spiritual path, each session representing a lesson along the initiatory journey we are living.

As students embarking on this initiatory path toward self-realization, we are sure to encounter difficulties and commit errors. The mistakes we make, though sometimes serious, are simply mistakes or misses. Learning from our errors allows us to perfect our technique and master our art. Mastering the art allows us to continue to contribute our gifts to humanity.

Offering ourselves and the gift of our deepness to others, we participate in the evolutionary dance of existence. To dance, we must move. In the beginning, our movements are often unskillful, even clumsy. In the beginning, it is difficult to stay centered, connected, and flowing, conscious of the music, the movement, the other, and the purpose. We encounter the same problems when we begin to learn the dance of intuitive readings and healings. As is their nature, problems have a tendency to sneak up on us and take us by surprise.

Even our marvelous intuitive self can be overwhelmed (temporarily) by the events occurring during a session we conduct on ourselves or with someone else. Very often, we will only gain awareness of what has happened after the event, when things have calmed down. It is during these moments, when we gain insight and lucidity as to how we function, that we really begin to learn about and understand ourselves. To advance, it is imperative that we accept the fact that we are bound to make mistakes. Once we have made mistakes, it is equally imperative that we learn from them and that we forgive ourselves for having made them. If we cannot forgive ourselves, we will limit our capacity to continue to move forward on our evolutionary path, thereby cutting ourselves off from the source that nourishes and teaches.

The greatest potential problems we encounter when we begin to exercise our intuition on others are the problems of projection, power, prediction, and interpretation. We shall take a look at each one of these potential "performance monsters," to better understand how and why they present a problem in the intuitive work.

PROJECTION

Projection is the process of transferring your personal reality onto someone else, while assuming that the other perceives, experiences and interprets reality in the same way that you do. Projection is based on the assumption that the other has exactly the same criteria for experience that you do. In fact, when you project onto somebody else, the other ceases to exist in their own right. All that exists is you, with your criteria, which you transfer onto the other. Projection is a widespread phenomenon to which we are all subjected on a daily basis to a greater or lesser extent, depending on our associations.

Projections are not necessarily harmful; in fact, they are often quite innocent. However to be the victim of a projection can be anything from irritating to infuriating, depending on the quality of the projection. In normal life, where we are constantly subjected to the projections of others, we can learn to be tolerant and more or less detached. People project unconsciously. Once we understand that they do this without being aware of what they are doing, we realize we have a choice either to confront them or to let them be. It is often simpler to let them be. If we choose the path of confrontation, we quickly discover that we spend a huge amount of time correcting judgments directed toward us in the form of social conversation. If we pay attention to ourselves in action, we have to admit that we also contribute our fair share of projections to the collective unconscious of humanity.

Some Examples of Projection in Action:

*Let me get you a glass of cold water. On a hot day like this
    I'm sure you prefer cold water.*
*I shall close the window. The breeze is a real nuisance for
    us all.*
I cannot talk to you. You are closed and unavailable.
You don't understand me. Nobody understands me.
*I won't give you salad. I know you absolutely detest it. You
    never eat it.*
You always say that.
*I won't even ask you if want to go for a walk, because you
    never want to go. You hate walking.*
You like all the same things I do.
*I hate rooms decorated in tones of orange. Nobody could
    possibly be comfortable in this room.*
I'm sure you'll love this dress. I adore it.
Because of you, I am sad, happy, angry . . .

Social projection can be irritating, but we learn to live with it. The best defense against projection is to be aware when it is happening and not to be "taken in" by it.

We can identify projection by the feeling it creates within us. In front of the person who is expressing their projection, we do not seem to exist at all. The other does not ask our opinion, but rather informs us who we are, how we behave, and why we behave the way we do. There is no discussion, only assumption. Faced with the projection of another, we often feel called to defend ourselves, justify ourselves, and state categorically that we are not the way they think we are. We may feel judged, limited, and smothered, finding ourselves allocated to a framework of perception that does not relate to who we are at all.

When we find ourselves reacting by stating "No, I'm not like that" or "No, I don't feel like that," or "No, I don't see things like that," we can be relatively sure we are experiencing someone's projections.

In intuitive work, projection manifests when we fall into the trap of jumping to conclusions. When we assume that "somebody is like this or that" because we or somebody else we know experienced something similar, we can easily project this assumption onto another without verifying with our intuition before we speak. Projection is a function of the rational mind, a habit of logic, and has absolutely no place in intuitive work. When we apply our intuition to the task of working on someone else, we must never assume that we know the other and never presume to understand the whys, hows, and whens of their various preoccupations. To assume and presume gives reign to the logical mind, severely limiting the scope of the intuitive capacity.

The act of projection is the act of sending something somewhere. It is true that, when we practice readings and healings, we must project our consciousness, our intuitive awareness, into the reality of the person on whom we are practicing. We "leave" our personal reality to step into the subjective reality of the other for a short period of time. What we must learn to do with clarity and precision, is to project our awareness without projecting our subjective reality at the same time. If we are centered in our rational mind and we project our awareness into the reality of the other, we take our personal subjective reality with us as we go, thus entering into the trap of projection. In this instance our reality is superimposed on the reality of the other and we assume that the reality we are perceiving is the reality of the other, when in fact, it is our own. In these cases, we can be surprised at how much like ourselves we find others!

The only effective way to avoid projection is to be sure that you are totally centered in intuitive mode before beginning to project awareness into the reality of the other. It is imperative to take all the time you need for your ritual of preparation before beginning the session and then, periodically during the session, take the time to come back to yourself, to your center. A good intuitive practitioner is like a good detective, always asking questions, never jumping to conclusions, determined to know the truth, and not stopping till the truth is uncovered.

When we begin to practice intuitive readings, we have a tendency to pass through a phase of projecting onto others. Initially it can be difficult to attain and maintain a sufficiently deep trance state, free of mental interference. There is also a type of inner cleansing that occurs, as though we must clean the filters of our perceptions, filters that are clogged with the unfinished business of our own personal history. Looking at others, we see reflections of ourselves and are reminded of our own past, our own problems. Distracted by the mental contemplation of our own inner stories, we quickly lose our centered state of intuitive detachment, returning to the level of consciousness of our personality and, from there, easily entering into the trap of projection. After a period of practice, combined with inner personal clearing work, we go beyond the problems of projection. We learn to recognize the symptoms within ourselves, signs that tell us we are losing our centeredness, our intuitive perspective, and the tone of voice which corresponds to the functioning of our intuitive mode of being. Then we can gently bring ourselves back to the correct inner state through which to work.

Projection is always an easier trap to fall into when we are working on someone already known to us. The advantage of group work is that we can practice on virtual strangers, people about whom we have very few preconceptions before we begin. When we know someone intimately, we are familiar with how they function, their problems, and their preoccupations. We also have the habit of interacting with them on a rational level of rapport. All this can make it quite difficult to avoid projecting on them. Family and friends present a delicate problem in this regard. When we wish to practice intuitive readings, it is natural that the people we practice on in the beginning will be our friends, family, or perhaps work associates. These people have preconceived ideas about us, just as we have conclusive opinions, judgments, and ideas about them. To succeed in practicing an intuitive reading, we are obliged to go beyond the normal level of social rapport we have established with these people. It is our responsibility in this instance to transform the relationship and create a new level of communication, a new level of meeting, which occurs at a much deeper, more essential, and more intimate level of contact. It is in these initial practice sessions that we are most likely to fall into the traps of projection. If we do, we find that the reading "lacks something," and that "something" will be a quality of depth, the atmosphere of profound contact that is experienced between two people when they meet beyond the superficial level of normal social contact.

If we succeed in creating the atmosphere of intuitive contact that is our objective, we often experience a transformation in the relationship with the person on whom we are practicing. Going beyond preconceived ideas and touching and exploring the subjective reality of the other, we can truly meet the other in the totality of their being.

This meeting is most often a heart-opening experience, creating renewed compassion, understanding, and respect for the other. In this regard, practicing on friends and family can become a healing and transformational experience for all involved.

The problem of projection teaches us very quickly that every person has their own subjective reality, their own criteria for experiences, and their own filter through which they perceive external reality. When we project, we limit the other, constricting them within our own subjective interpretation of reality. Limited by our imposed structures, others must struggle to be themselves in front of us. Often, they will choose distance, separating from us so that they can feel free to be themselves. Once we have understood the limiting system of projection and its fundamentally distasteful consequences to ourselves and others, we have good reason to go beyond it as a habitual and often unconscious behavior. When we cease to impose our projections on others and simply create a space in which others can be themselves, we are finally free to discover the other in their authenticity, their spontaneity, and their truth. Going beyond projection, we become free to perceive the intrinsic movement of existence, both in ourselves and in others. It is in this essential movement, the energetic dance of light and matter, that we touch the truth and can perceive the true nature of ourselves and others.

POWER

The trap of power is the trap of domination over others. We dominate by manipulating and creating relationships of dependence, where others become victims and we, the controller. "Power-tripping" can be very subtle in its behavioral manifestation, or it can be quite clumsy and blatant. The most common trap of power in the intuitive work is the process of creating a relationship of dependence, where the client is obliged to always be the client, coming to the practitioner for information and healing. In this type of relationship, the client loves, respects, perhaps even worships the practitioner and, in the extreme, consults the practitioner before making even the smallest decision. The practitioner, basking in the recognition of their considerable powers, forgets that their original purpose was to empower others to heal themselves. Teaching others to contact their own intuition so they can become their own teacher/healer is to give them their independence and ultimate freedom. Relationships of dependence are relationships of manipulation, and relationships of this nature do not have a place in the sacred work of intuition development.

We must always remember to encourage others to come back to themselves and find their own inner resources for healing. When others compliment us for our powers of perception and healing, we must remember, after having graciously accepted the compliment, to remind them that they too, have this capacity within themselves, just waiting to be developed to its full potential.

Power, in itself, is a healthy and essential quality, assisting us to assert and affirm who we are. Our power allows us to penetrate, create, and transform. With our power we destroy, we terminate and undo our creations once they are no longer useful to us. Thanks to our personal power, we dare to be ourselves, we dare to assume we have something to give to existence. The danger of power lies in the temptation to abuse it. If we are not clear about our limits, if we lack respect for the limits of others, we can project our power in such a way that we trespass on their integrity and their sacred space. We must be vigilant about our power, never underestimating "the power of our power." When we practice using our intuitive skills, we find ourselves in a position of great power. Others give us permission to penetrate with our intuitive awareness into their reality, into their sacred space, even into the deepness of their own souls. We must go with great respect, with great precision, and with enormous awareness, so that they do not feel violated or betrayed by our coming. Our ultimate purpose is to aid others to open, to flower, and to empower themselves. If we can show them that we can exercise our own power with elegance, restraint, and precision, respecting their limits as well as encouraging them to go beyond them, we will be serving as a valuable role model to the other.

Words which can indicate the existence of power games in action are "should, must, always, never."

> *You should change your behavior because . . .*
> *You must be more courageous.*
> *You should not continue to act like a victim.*
> *You must see the truth.*
> *You should be more aware.*
> *You must listen to me.*
> *You will never be strong enough to succeed.*
> *You should always exercise and eat sensibly.*
> *You should not eat meat.*
> *You must not act in this way.*

It is a basic and essential rule in intuitive readings not to use the word "should." Do not presume to tell someone something in an absolute way. No commands, no absolutes, no orders. You can give your intuitive opinion from a position of personal empowerment without becoming a fascist dictator. Our objective is to share our intuitive impressions in such a way that others can explore their options with greater perspective, free to choose for themselves the path which is most appropriate for them.

PREDICTIONS

The philosophy of intuitive development supports the belief that we are the creators of our own reality, incarnated to realize our destiny while working toward the fulfillment of a certain purpose or mission.

There are many possible ways to arrive at the realization of this purpose, and there are many choices we have to make along the path. We are free beings and nothing, apart from our essential objective at the beginning, is predetermined. As souls, we have also chosen to assume certain karmic obligations. These obligations will cause certain other souls to arrive in our lives, souls with whom we shall have to deal with in one way or another to honor the obligations. We will experience the consequences of our actions in relationship to others as we travel the path of our lives. Our ultimate freedom lies in the fact that we can act and react as we choose in every given moment of our lives. There is no predetermined, fatalistic path that we are obliged to follow. We have a choice, and the exercise of this capacity for choice is essential to the development of our soul, as well as to the evolution of our being. In fact, we have a sort of karmic invitation to accept the responsibility to choose and therefore consciously determine the direction of our evolution. When we allow another to choose for us, we give to the other the responsibility for our lives, thus rendering ourselves impotent and without place, a victim.

The trap of offering predictions is the trap of the power game. Telling others what will happen to them robs them of their power to create their life for themselves, rendering them impotent in front of the possibilities of life. Predictions serve as a form of programming for the unconscious mind. If we are led to believe in the truth of a prediction, it will quite possibly realize itself, as our unconscious mind will work to create it. This is not such a problematic phenomenon when a prediction is "positive" and we receive a programming that directs us unconsciously toward a "happy ending." However, too often, predictive work is "gloom and doom stuff," horror stories of suffering, failure, and disappointment, exactly the kind of forecasts on which fear feeds and from which it grows fat. The popular caricature of the clairvoyant that we know from films, fiction, and fantasy—the fortune-teller, gypsy woman, and eccentric psychic—has a well-known reputation for telling the future. Because of this predictive orientation, the more sacred aspect of intuitive work has been largely lost and the work itself almost totally discredited. In fact, it is not very difficult to tell someone their "future." With our intuitive awareness, we can perceive others as they function in their daily life and we can gain intuitive access to their hopes and fears, their projects and dreams. Perceiving their psychological nature and their usual pattern of behavior, we can with reasonable ease "predict" the possible scenario of the rest of their lives. If they continue to behave in the same fashion, without making decisions or choosing conscious change, their life will unfold in a largely "predictable" pattern. With a client who is open and vulnerable, it is possible to plant the program of "gloom and doom," "health and happiness," "loss and gain," "death and depression," or "fortune and goodwill." Predictive work is not true intuitive work, it is simply a "psychic circus act," an entertainment show, and more importantly an often unconscious power game.

It is true that, with our intuition, we can perceive possible future scenarios. It is also true that we can experience flashes of what may seem to be the future, but these are only possibilities. We have the power to go toward one possibility or to choose another preferred possibility. It is our choice, our birthright, to create the reality of our choosing.

To fall into the trap of prediction is to fall into a deep trap of self-delusion, domination, and manipulation. People may ask you to tell them their future. It can be a great temptation to fulfill their desire, to please them, and to soothe their fears by telling them what you perceive through exercising your powers of intuition. Be aware of the temptation—it is one of the greatest traps you can face.

We must remember that there is no greater power than the power of the truth. One great truth is that we are the creators of our own destinies. All that we create, we can transform. We are totally responsible for the creation of our lives. As intuitive readers, we can offer no greater gift to others than the gift of their own creative power. If we can help others to see and understand that their path is their own to sculpt and create as they feel and as they choose, we are then truly working in our capacity as healers. In the philosophy of intuition development, prediction has no place, as it is contrary to the sacred truths of freedom, evolution, and individual choice. Somebody who practices predictive work is not practicing intuitive work in the sacred sense of its original purpose as a catalyst for spiritual evolution. Therefore, at all costs, avoid the trap. If others ask you to tell them what their future holds for them, ask them what they would like it to hold and help them to explore the possible futures of their lives. Help them to find within themselves the resources they need which will empower them to create their lives and manifest their dreams. Help them to become responsible for the lives they are living in the here and now, so that they can more clearly choose their direction for the future. Discussing possibilities for the future is not at all the same thing as predicting the future. We must remember that the purpose of intuitive readings is to aid others in understanding who they are, where they are, and why they are where they are, here and now. This is already a large agenda for a session and more than enough to manage, especially when you begin to practice readings.

INTERPRETATION

When we utilize our intuition to gain information and insight into the state of another person, we receive the responses to our questions in several possible forms: as direct perception, as symbolic images, as words, as feelings (emotional resonances), or as sensations. The more we develop our intuitive capacity, the more we will receive information at all these levels of possible function—as an image, with words, feeling, sensation, and a sense of knowingness. With practice and experience, and with familiarization of the intuitive process, the art of asking, receiving, and communicating in intuitive mode becomes second nature, a state into which we slip simply and naturally.

In the beginning of practice, we are grateful to receive any response from our intuition and we are relieved that the response is clear enough that we can communicate it to someone else in answer to their questions. As beginners, we are not yet able to apply ourselves comfortably to the art of interpretation, which is, in itself, a sophisticated and subtle challenge, demanding time, patience, and lots of practice. Once we become familiar with the functioning of our intuition and begin to understand the way it communicates to us, we will naturally begin to understand the messages contained within the information given.

The art of interpretation rests in the delicate balance between saying too much or too little, becoming too concrete or staying too much in the symbolic. A symbolic image can be a powerful catalyst, full of meaning and justice for the person to whom it is offered. It can also be received as a somewhat vague message, saying something, but nothing very precise or particular.

Our challenge when we work with the symbolism of the intuition, is to give a concrete sense to the information we receive, without rendering it so solid that we create a limitation for the person with whom we are communicating. We must allow the symbol room to breathe and speak to the unconscious of our partner, trusting that if we have received this particular information it is because it is appropriate for the person with whom we are working. It is not necessary for us, as intuitive readers, to logically understand the sense of the message in order for it to have a sense for our partner. It is always comforting to feel we understand, but we must remember that understanding at this level is comprehension by the logical mind. On an intuitive level, we can often "feel" the truth of the information, while at a conscious level, we cannot see or understand its relevance at all. In the case where we give a reading and do not particularly understand the information we receive, we can be pleased, as in this instance we know it is our intuition functioning and not the logical mind. We can be assured that we are in relation with the other at a level of deepness that corresponds to intuitive function.

The most common problem we encounter in regard to interpretation is one of trying to interpret with the logical mind, rather than allowing the intuitive self to explain the meaning of the information received. We must trust that the intuition has all the resources it needs to explain to us the relevance of one symbol or another and we must, above all, remember to ask our intuition to interpret for us.

In the beginning, we have a tendency to stay in intuitive mode long enough to receive the information and communicate it, at which point, we let go with a great sigh of successful relief, come out of trance, and begin to discuss with our partner the possible meaning of the information received. It is really much simpler, more interesting, and much more pertinent to stay in trance, ask our intuition, and communicate the response. Then we can come out of our inner state and share the results together.

In order to master the art of interpretation, you must be willing to continually question your intuition, until you have, within yourself, the intuitive sense of the meaning of the information received in relation to the original question of your partner. Very often, when your intuition gives you an image as a response, you will need to begin to describe the image to the other before you begin to feel the sense and relevance of it in relation to the question asked. It is as though the image must begin to move and you, with your intuitive awareness, must begin to move within the image before it can come fully to life and express its sense to you as words and feelings.

If we interpret information with our logical mind, we discover that we are again faced with the problem of projection—putting our concept of reality onto someone else, rather than stepping into their reality. Interpretation done by logic may appear accurate, but it will be dry, cold, and lacking in feeling for the person who faces it.

If you have difficulties receiving interpretations from your intuition, simply describe what you receive and allow your partners to interpret the sense of the message for themselves. In more advanced intuitive training, the art of interpretation is dealt with in depth and precision, as it is an indispensable aspect of intuitive work. However, for the reading and healing exercises that follow as practical teaching aids, you will find that the symbolic images have a tendency to interpret themselves. After your reading, you can ask your partners how they relate the information to their daily lives. The feedback you receive will help you enormously to understand the meaning and sense behind the messages you have received from your intuition. In this way, you will advance slowly but surely along the path of accurate interpretation.

The Sacred Healing Power of Presence and Silence

The intuitive state is above all, a state of inner presence and silence. Entering into communion with ourselves, with our deepness, and with our truth, we can simply be. In the emptiness of inner silence, we find peace and, paradoxically, the fullness of the plenitude of our being. From a state of inner presence, we commune with nature, with light, and with the universe. We can also enter into communion with the deepness of another and reflect back to them the truth of how we perceive them in their deepness. When we give an intuitive reading, words are the tools we use to communicate the perceptions we receive on an intuitive level. Words have a tremendous power and, thanks to them, we can share our perceptions. But we must also remember the power of silence, the power of atmosphere, and the power of presence as healing tools.

When we are centered and silent in our intuitive mode, we radiate a very particular atmosphere, an atmosphere of calm, of centeredness, and of presence. This atmosphere will unconsciously help our partners to find this same state of being within themselves, whether they are consciously searching for it or not. In a reading session, there are many things we will say that will touch the heart and soul of the person to whom we are speaking. In the moments of silence between words, the person will be touched in another way and this touch, the touch of silence, of presence, will also bring healing, solace, and hope. In moments of silence, a deep communion can happen, a meeting of being with being. For this reason, do not be afraid of silence. Rather welcome it, knowing that even in moments of silence healing is happening.

When you give a reading to another, take the time to prepare yourself. Take all the time you need; five to ten minutes is not too long. Accept your need to be silent, to return to the silent place of your deepness, the silent presence of your intuition, before you begin asking questions and offering answers. Do not consider silence to be a sign of a weakness on your part. Rather, perceive it as a strength, as an integral part of the session and as a balance between moments of dialogue shared with the other.

In silence, there is a transmission that occurs, going beyond words, straight to the heart of the other. In silence, we find the sacred atmosphere of the temple and in this atmosphere we find true healing.

INTUITION AND COMMUNICATION

Words have tremendous power. Intuition, as a vehicle for truth, requires words if the truth is to be shared in the form of communication. There is an art to communicating intuitive truth in a manner that can be heard, understood, and integrated by the receiver. Communicating with diplomacy, simplicity, and grace can create profound and permanent healing, while careless communication can create confusion, defensiveness, and even deep psychological damage.

As an intuitive person, it is important to respect the limits of an individual, sharing information received to the extent that you feel it is useful. Too much information, even when of a high quality, can create a state of confusion and imbalance. You must learn to witness the impact of your words as you work by intuitively maintaining a perception of the state of availability of your partners. You can feel their state of receptivity with your clairsentient capacity or perceive clairvoyantly by observing the changes in their subtle energy state as you work. When and if they reach saturation point, you can begin to terminate the session, allowing them to digest and integrate the information received at their own pace.

There are several basic rules and essential tools for communication used throughout most counseling disciplines, which are appropriate to learn and practice when you work with your intuition on others.

1. *Speaking/Listening:* Listen to what your client says to you. To be a good speaker you need to be a good listener. By really listening, you will better understand the needs of your client and address those needs in your reading.

2. *Speaking for Yourself:* Always speak for yourself—"I am, I feel, I sense, I see," etc. Accept responsibility for the position, the place, you are assuming and speak directly from this place.

3. *Creating Rapport:* Use mirroring tools for assisting your client to relax and feel at ease in your presence. Be aware of body posture, gestures, and expressions of your client, giving you keys through which you can establish a rapport of trust and willingness in the session.

POINTS TO REMEMBER

When you are giving an intuitive reading remember the following points:

1. There is always a positive intention behind every thought and action. Look for this intention, as it will lead you to the essence of the issue you are reading.

2. Balance your information with strengths and weaknesses, positives and negatives.

3. Behind every difficult experience is a possible valuable gain.

4. Use your diplomacy, especially when speaking about difficult and delicate subjects.

5. Understand the level of your client. Ask your intuition to tell you the level of the information they need and then choose your language appropriately so that the other can understand you.

6. Interpret your metaphors. When you receive a symbolic image as a metaphor, describe it accurately. This symbol may speak very clearly to your client. However, also interpret it, bring it to reality, adapt it to the framework of daily life.

7. Never tell a person what they should do. Present options and possibilities and explore possible outcomes, but do not predict the future of your clients.

8. Accept that you may not personally understand some of the information you receive from your intuition. Stay in trust.

9. Always consult your intuition during a session when you have a question to ask. Do not consult your logical mind.

10. Remember that all information exchanged in a session of intuitive reading is totally confidential. Respect your partner's privacy.

CHAPTER SEVENTEEN

The Practice of Readings

The following four reading models will allow you to practice using your intuitive abilities with family and friends.

We begin with readings using symbolic images and from there progress to readings where we explore the state of the subtle or energetic body. Finally, relationship readings create the possibility of exploring the dynamics existing between two people, with a view to clarifying and transforming problematic aspects of the relationship.

Symbolic readings can be considered the most "simple" readings, providing a base of experience that allows us to progress to more sophisticated styles of reading as we gain confidence. The Tree reading, though simple, is highly useful and may be a moving experience for the recipient. This is the first reading undertaken by students in the intuition training and one I also use to train my advanced students to perfect their technique.

We follow exactly the same steps as in the Tree meditation, the only difference being that someone other than you is the subject. For this exercise, therefore, you will need a willing partner.

Tree Reading

Recommended time: 30 minutes.

- Follow all the steps of preparation and when you feel ready, imagine your partner (who is sitting in front of you) comes to your Temple and enters inside, sitting in front of you, inside your sacred working space.

- Inform your intuitive self that you wish to do an intuitive reading of this person, working through the symbolic image of a tree and ask your intuition to show you the image which corresponds to the truth of the state of your partner.

- Allow the image of the tree to appear, and explore the image . . . regard the tree from a distance, noting its size, its shape,

Figure 17. The posture for giving an intuitive reading.

and the environment surrounding the tree, becoming aware of the atmosphere of the image you are perceiving.

- In the same way that you have explored the tree in your own personal tree meditation, allow your intuition to guide you in exploring the symbolic tree of your partner. Perceive the environment, the soil, the water, and the Sun . . . perceive the trunk, the roots, the branches, and the leaves of the tree . . . being aware of the atmosphere and being aware of how you feel in your body as you perceive the various aspects of the tree.

- Describe what you are perceiving to your partner, and allow the images to speak to the other.

- When you have described the images, ask what the tree lacks and what the tree needs to be well, to be healed.

- Share this information with your partner.

- When you feel that your reading is finished, you may ask your partner if he or she has any questions with regards to the information you have received. Staying centered and grounded, allow your intuitive self to answer the questions. If your intuitive self does not give a response to the questions, simply inform your partner that you do not have an answer to the question.

- When you feel the session is over, say good-bye to the person in your Temple and imagine them leaving your inner Temple.

- Take a few minutes to stay quietly with yourself, being centered, present, and connected to light.

- When you feel ready, open your eyes.

- Take some time to speak together about the experience.

House Reading

Recommended time: 45 minutes.

- Prepare yourself by following all the steps of preparation and, when you feel ready, imagine that your partner (who is sitting in front of you) comes into your Temple and sits down facing you.

- Inform your intuitive self that you wish to give an intuitive reading working through the symbolic image of a house and ask your intuition to show you the image of a house which corresponds to the truth of the inner state of your partner.

- Allow the image of the house to appear and begin to explore the image with your intuitive perception . . . Perceive the exterior of the house in as much detail as possible and discover the doorway through which you can gain entry . . . prepare yourself to enter and continue to explore in the same manner you have explored the house that represented you in the house meditation . . .

- Inside the house, you will find four rooms, representing the physical, emotional, mental, and spiritual state of your partner. Taking your time, explore each one of these rooms, describing the images you receive to your partner as they are offered to you by your intuitive self. As you explore each room, be aware of the atmosphere you discover and the various objects you find in the rooms. Describe your perceptions in detail, allowing the images to speak to the other.

- When you have finished describing each room, you can ask your intuition to tell you what is lacking, what is needed, and what is appropriate for transformation and healing. Share this information with your partner.

- If your partner has questions related to the information you have received, allow yourself a few minutes to receive the intuitive response to the questions posed.

- When you feel that the reading is finished, imagine the other leaving your Temple and give yourself a few minutes, staying quietly with yourself, before you open your eyes and begin sharing about the experience with your partner.

Chakra Reading

Recommended time: 60 minutes.

- Close your eyes and prepare with the steps of preparation.

- Imagine your partner comes into your Temple and sits down facing you.

- Inform you intuitive self that you are going to do an intuitive reading of the chakras of your partner and ask your intuition to show you the chakras of your partner.

- Begin with the first chakra and finish with the seventh chakra, remembering the significance of each chakra from the chakra meditations you have practiced on yourself.

- For each of the seven chakras perceive . . . symbolic images describing the state of the chakra shapes, forms, colors . . . the atmosphere, feelings and emotions, the flow of energy in the chakra, blockages to the flow of energy in the chakra. Ask your intuition to guide you to perceive the actual state of each chakra, and ask to receive the quality that each chakra needs for transformation.

- Share the information that you receive with your partner as you receive it, finishing with each chakra before moving on to the next one.

- When you have finished reading the seven chakras, permit your partner to ask questions related to the information you have received during the reading.

- When you feel that the reading is complete, take the time to imagine your partner leaving your Temple. Take a few minutes to stay centered within yourself and when you feel ready, open your eyes. Take some time to share with your partner about the reading.

Relationship Reading

Recommended time: 30 minutes.

- Bring your partner into your Temple and imagine that the other person involved in the relationship comes along at the same time. Intuitively observe these two people together, and allow yourself to feel the atmosphere between them. How do they look at each other? How do they position themselves in relation to each other?

- Ask your intuition to guide you to perceive the truth of what is happening between these two people. You may pose the following questions (or some of them) to your intuition to assist you in exploring the dynamics of the relationship you are reading. What is essential in this relationship? What is the real problem? On each side? What does each person have to understand? What does each person have to teach the other? What does each person have to learn from the other? What does each person lack? What does each person need? What is the positive intention behind the conflict?

- Share the perceptions you receive with your partner, taking some time to answer questions, if there are some, and when you feel ready, finish the reading. Share together your experiences of the exchange.

CHAPTER EIGHTEEN

Intuition as a Healing Tool

The decision to develop our intuition, and the practice of utilizing it, trigger a profound reconciliation between the soul/spirit and the body/mind, realigning us with our connection to the universe and the sense of who we are, well beyond the dimension of our social personality. We rediscover the richness of our deepness and, very often for the first time, we discover a means through which we can express and share our wisdom and unconditional love with others. The inner movement of realignment of our axis, creating an energetic connection with the Earth and light and the insights and revelations we experience when we open to our intuitive selves, represent a considerable internal personal transformation. We feel reborn, full of hope and gratitude. We experience these transformations of inner reconciliation as a veritable healing, and we know from firsthand experience the healing power of the intuition. The discovery that we have the capacity to heal ourselves and transform our lives creates a spontaneous movement toward others. We have a natural desire to share what we have learned with others who are close to us and we may feel called to help others, to help them heal their problems and difficulties, to help them to rediscover their true and deep nature.

Using our intuition to help others allows us to develop qualities of tolerance, acceptance, and compassion toward the people with whom we work and permits us to practice the techniques we are slowly learning to master.

Applying our intuitive perception using the techniques of readings and healings allows us to show and share with others the truth of who we are, the truth of our gifts. Practicing on others allows us to advance rapidly. We learn to perceive more clearly, more deeply, and to communicate our impressions more precisely, with tact and respect for the other. When we practice on somebody else, we apply the same techniques as when we work on ourselves. However, we discover a different dynamic—the dynamic of two. We experience the dynamic of sharing, of exchange, and this quality of interaction favors transformation and healing.

To use intuition as a healing tool, we assess not only the current state of others, but also their lacks and needs. Once we have perceived what others need for healing, we transmit this quality to them using techniques of psychic healing, where we utilize the presence of light (prana) as a healing dynamic. Having already utilized this principle on ourselves during our meditation practice, we can begin to practice healing others with relative ease.

Before beginning to heal others, we must remember to respect the progressive steps of the intuitive reading process so that we are sure to have all the elements we need to succeed with the healing session. These steps are as follows:

1. *Assess the current state of being of the other:* Beginning with the question of the "patient," explore the problem intuitively, perceiving the dynamics of the problem, its repercussions and its origin.

2. *Become aware of what the other lacks/needs:* What is missing, what is needed to be well, to be healed, to be at peace? Ask your intuition to help you to perceive the true lack and, therefore, the true need of the other.

3. *Transmit the qualities needed:* Once you have explored the current state, the lack and the need, you are ready to begin the final part

of your healing session, in which you will use the imposition of your hands to send healing light, colors, and particular qualities to the person you wish to heal.

Even though the steps described here are simple, we always follow this progression when working with the intuition as a healing tool. Regardless of the complexity of the problem there is always a lack, a need, and a quality we can transmit to them using light, color, and the healing power of the heart.

CHAPTER NINETEEN

The Practice of Healing

The gift of healing is innate in us all, a birthright we can choose to utilize, if we so wish. Like all gifts of creative expression, some people have a larger innate talent than others and are therefore called more strongly to develop and explore their natural healing skills.

Once we begin to use our intuition to help others, we are already engaged on a path of healing. An intuitive reading, providing perspective, insight, and revelation to the person who receives it, is an experience of healing in itself and the transformation that follows shows us the healing power that words can have when they react in the world of matter. Truth, when spoken with the quality of compassion, creates an atmosphere of acceptance, and acceptance is the key to healing.

Intuitive readings give us information, insights, and clarification about ourselves, our problems, our path. Healings invite us to surrender, to accept, and to receive. In receiving a healing, we allow ourselves to receive love, energy, and light. We allow another to help us and we allow life energy to flow in us, bringing movement, fulfillment, and the sense of being cared for.

When we heal another, we act as intermediary between light and matter, heaven and Earth. Healing is a sacred work, a work of marrying light and matter and bringing these two opposite qualities into communion. We need to be open in our hearts—open to light, open to love, and open to ourselves, present and alert, aware and available. When we heal, we call the light and direct it with our consciousness to wherever we wish it to go, sending it with love to the person who is receiving.

There are several progressive steps involved in the process of healing and each step must be respected in order to master the art of healing others. The steps we follow are preparation, reception, transmission, and intention.

PREPARATION

We use the ritual of preparation to ensure we are well centered, grounded, and present before we begin a healing work on somebody else. Particular attention must be paid to the personal boundary and the vertical alignment, so that we are well connected to both Earth and light, balanced, present, and ready to give.

RECEPTION

We call the light from the universe to flow into us through the seventh chakra. It flows down into our heart chakra, where it mixes with the quality of compassion in the heart. From the chest, it flows down to the second chakra, into the belly. The light circulates in the lower belly and then rises, flowing back to the heart. From the heart chakra, the light energy flows to our arms and down through the arms to our hands. We receive the light into our hands as a flowing, liquid, healing heat.

TRANSMISSION

From our hands we transmit the healing light to our partner, either by placing our hands directly on the part of the body where healing is needed or by sending it a certain distance from the physical body. We transmit the light which has traveled through our body, to the body of the other, directing the passage of the light with our consciousness.

INTENTION

We use our will, our power, to "steer" the light to the zone of the body where it is needed, imagining that the other is receiving and integrating the light we are sending in the most appropriate way. We maintain concentration in this manner, until we feel that the light has reached its destination and has been absorbed and integrated into the energy system of the person to whom we are sending. While sending light, we maintain contact with our deep intention that this healing intervention be an intervention of love, given to create transformation and evolution in the other. We hold within ourselves the intention that the light we are transmitting be offered for the highest good of all the beings involved. With this intention we can be sure that we shall never unconsciously harm someone with whom we are working.

Intention is a quality which gives power to the healing intervention, causing the light to penetrate the density of matter, finding its correct destination with efficiency and precision.

When we heal from a position of vertical alignment, we are naturally centered in trust and certainty. It is our inner certainty of the justice of our healing strategy which gives us the clear intention we need to follow the healing through from beginning to end, creating a transformation in the person we are healing.

HEALING TREATMENTS

Channeling Light to the Heart

Ask your partner to lie down comfortably on his or her back, covered, if necessary, to create a feeling of warmth and security. You may wish to use a cushion under the knees and/or head. Ask your partner to simply relax, breathing in a rhythm that feels easy and natural.

- Take yourself through the ritual of preparation, imagining that your partner arrives in your Temple and lies down comfortably in front of you. Bring your attention to the crown of your head and imagine your seventh chakra as a sphere of energy opening toward the sky. Expand the sphere, opening it wider and wider, and imagine your axis as a large column of light, as large as the size of your body.

- Imagine light, warm loving light, healing light, white light, intelligent light, present and pure, and call the light to you.

- The light descends and flows into you through the crown of your head, flowing like liquid, flowing into you, down through your axis and into your chest, into your heart and from your heart, the light flows down, down into your belly, into the sphere of your second chakra. Imagine the light flowing into your belly, feel the light filling your belly, white light flowing into you, flowing up now, up toward your heart, into your heart and from your heart, two rivers of light flowing to your arms and filling your arms with light, flowing down to your hands and filling your hands . . . warming, filling, overflowing with light, liquid light flowing, white light filling your hands, hands full of light.

- When you feel ready, place your hands on the heart chakra of your partner, staying in connection with the pathway of the light, light flowing from your head to your heart, from your

Figure 18. Transmitting healing qualities: channeling light to the heart.

heart to your belly, from your belly to your heart, from your heart to your arms, from your arms to your hands . . . and from your hands to the heart of the other.

- Send light into the heart chakra of your partner, imagining the heart chakra as a sphere of energy, a sphere receiving and filling with light. The light fills the heart, and from the heart will flow throughout the subtle body to wherever it is needed.

- Be aware of the light flowing into you, flowing through you and flowing into and through your partner . . . continue to send light for several minutes until you feel intuitively that your treatment is finished.

- When you feel ready, gently and slowly remove your hands from the chest of your partner, bringing them back into your lap. Continue to receive light, allowing light to fill you and flow in you. Place your hands on your own heart, replenishing yourself with light. Maintain this posture for a couple of minutes and then, gently let go of your inner concentration and simply rest.

- Take the time to share with your partner the impressions and feelings you have both experienced during the healing treatment.

Channeling Colors to the Heart

- Following all the steps of preparation, bring white light into your hands.

- When you feel ready, ask the light to become red light and imagine the light as a red river, flowing into you and through you, filling your hands with the energy and atmosphere of red. Place your hands on, or just above, the first chakra of your partner and imagine the chakra as a sphere, as an empty receptacle. Begin to fill the sphere with red liquid light, picturing the level of liquid rising until it reaches the top. After a few minutes the sphere will be full.

- Remove your hands and, resting quietly within yourself, ask the light to become orange, imagining orange light now. Place your hands over the second chakra of your partner and fill the second chakra with orange liquid light, taking a few minutes to accomplish your task.

- Repeat this procedure for each of the colors that relate to each of the chakras . . . yellow for the third chakra, green for the fourth chakra, blue for the fifth chakra, purple for the sixth chakra, white for the seventh chakra.

- When you have filled each chakra with the colored liquid light corresponding to it, gently remove yourself from contact with your partner. Continue to imagine light flowing into you and place your hands on your heart chakra to re-source yourself for a few minutes.

- When you feel ready, relax your inner awareness, and bring the treatment to an end.

- Take the time to share with your partner the impressions you have both experienced during the treatment.

Channeling Qualities

- Follow all the steps of personal preparation.

- Bring your partner into your Temple, and sit facing each other. . . . Ask your intuition to give you three qualities that this person needs to receive and three places in the body where they are needed. Trust the response you receive.

- When you feel ready, call the light. When you feel the light is present and flowing, begin to imagine the first quality . . . imagine the quality as a color, a feeling, a sound, an atmosphere . . . imagine the quality as fully as you can, allowing yourself to feel this quality deeply, to embody and then radiate this quality.

- Send the quality out through your hands, placing your hands on the zone of the body of your partner where the quality is needed and imagine the quality flowing into the body, flowing and filling this zone of the body with the quality which is needed. Continue to imagine the quality as clearly as you can, seeing it, feeling it, hearing it, being it, imagine you are this quality and the light is this quality and the quality is flowing into the body of your partner, fulfilling the need and bringing healing . . .

Figure 19. Transmitting healing qualities: channeling qualities to the belly.

- After some minutes, finish sending the first quality and bring your attention to the second quality, imagining this quality with all your senses . . .

- Repeat the procedure for the second and third qualities, transmitting the qualities to the part of the body where they are needed . . .

- Take as much time as you feel you need and when you feel, intuitively, that you are finished, bring your treatment to completion, taking the time to share together your impressions.

6

INTUITION AND
EVOLUTION OF
THE SOUL

CHAPTER TWENTY

Past Lives and Reincarnation

Once embarked on a path of research into the essential nature of ourselves, it quickly becomes evident that we are much more than we seem to be. Access to our intuition opens us to the vast dimensions of our inner worlds. Reconciliation with our deepest selves, with our souls, delivers us to the experience of our capacity to perceive and understand the timeless realms of the universe existing beyond the concrete world of daily life. Going beyond the sense of ourselves as beings defined solely through reference to a body and personality, we find our place in a larger framework of existence.

The inner work of meditation and contemplation in which we engage brings a dimension of sharpened lucidity and heightened sensitivity into our fundamental way of perceiving reality. Exploration into the nature of our intuitive selves reveals to us the many faces of our personalities, at the same time leading us to the eventual discovery of our original face. Within our souls we find evidence of the long path of evolution we have already traveled and we can trace the path with our consciousness, reliving past lives, remembering past deaths, and recalling the process of rebirth we have experienced many, many times.

As we purify the body/mind and raise our consciousness with the regular practice of inner contemplation, we release ourselves from the stories of the past, a liberation that touches both our current lives and the lives of our previous incarnations. As we become more and more familiar with the function of our energetic bodies, we discover that we can have ready access to past life memories which are recorded and stored in the chakra system of our subtle energy body.

Healing ourselves with light in a certain chakra during sessions of meditation, we can find ourselves confronted with the scenario of an unresolved past life problem that has certain relevance to the actual state of being of the chakra we are in the process of healing. Accepting, exploring, and releasing the feelings evoked by the material that has been evoked in the session, we effectively liberate ourselves from old unfinished business that has a karmic weight attached to it. Freeing ourselves from the past, we are more available to the present moment and more able to assume our current responsibilities with a light heart and clear consciousness.

In the same way that we can access information about past lives within ourselves, we can use our intuition to give past-life readings to others. Once we have learned how to gain access to the deepness of others and enter into communication with their deepness, we can explore past incarnations, researching the relationship between current life difficulties and unresolved trauma from previous lives.

Once we have identified the precise nature of the problem being experienced in this life, we invite our intuitive awareness to reveal the past incarnation that has relevance to the current problem. We are able to perceive the life scenario in which the other was "entangled" and the elements which have remained unresolved. Very often, we find scenarios in which complex relational problems were difficult to clarify and solve, thus remaining unresolved during a period of several lifetimes. Eventually, the wheel of evolutionary movement brings the beings involved in the unresolved problem back into a personal relationship in their current lives. A similar type of problem establishes itself in the relationship and all parties are faced with the possibility of resolving and going beyond their habitual manner of relating and interacting.

Guided by the wisdom and perspective of the intuition, it is possible to help others perceive and understand the difficult dynamics they are facing in relationships with others. From a perspective of evolution, it becomes possible to consider problems as necessary challenges for the development of the soul. Accepting the problem as an occasion for personal growth, it is easier to accept the other with whom we are experiencing difficulties in this life and to whom we were attached in another.

Healing a relationship problem with another allows us to continue to heal our relationship with ourselves. Freeing ourselves from the tangled web of the unfinished business of past lives assists us to come to relationships in our current life with greater availability. When we are weighed down in the deepness of our being with unresolved past-life problems, we have a tendency to react unconsciously because of the unfinished business from the past resting between ourselves and the other. Unknown to ourselves, we react in a habitual manner to the other, even though we have no logical reason for doing so in this life. Behavior is expressed that cannot be explained and is often quite baffling. Strong emotions are evoked that have no concrete bearing on the actual present-life situation.

• Case Study •

I receive a client who has recently met and fallen in love with a man. This couple have decided to build their lives together. It is a period of pleasure and joy for them both—a new beginning full of promise, plans, and a rich and unfolding affair of the heart. However, my client is possessed by a terrible foreboding fear that she will lose her man. Her fear is inconsistent with the atmosphere of the actual situation. Every time they part, even if the parting will only be for a short period of time, she becomes possessed by the certainty that her lover is disappearing forever.

She finds herself clinging to him, afraid to let him go, terrified that he will abandon her and never return. Her fear is illogical. Her lover wants nothing more than to spend as much time as possible with her. The situation is difficult to manage, creating drama and conflict within the relationship and evoking a terrible suffering in my client, who is facing the problem of her fear of abandonment without much success.

When we explore the problem in an individual session and I give her an intuitive past-life reading, I find her living in medieval England in a small village. She is a young woman and has known her current love in this past life as a beloved with whom she would like to live her life. However, before they can establish a life together, her boyfriend is conscripted and must leave to help defend the people of the region from invaders.

He never returns. Brokenhearted she awaits him, but she is never to see him again. Even though his death in battle is eventually confirmed, she cannot accept his death. She continues to await his return, mourning his absence, but never his death. With the passing of time she resumes her life, but she never frees herself from the sorrow of his absence and the sense of having been abandoned.

In the session, we work with this information and the correspondence it has to the feelings she is experiencing in this life. The paradox of deep joy and fear she is living in relationship to her boyfriend takes on a deeper sense. She recognizes her fear of abandonment as having been a common thread throughout several meaningful relationships in her life. By being able to grieve for her lost love of another life, she is at last able to let go of this old trauma and become available to live the pleasure of the reunion she is experiencing through their renewed meeting.

• • •

Awareness of past lives and the capacity to engage in a transformational work about them, can also assist us to heal ourselves of irrational fears and phobias which we cannot explain.

• *Case Study* •

I have always been afraid of the water. When I was a youngster, we often went to the beach on the weekends and for extended holidays. My brothers and sisters would plunge into the water with total abandon, while I stayed at the edge watching them play among themselves. I was anxious, worried for their safety, and incapable of abandoning myself to the water. The sight of the waves rolling into the shore filled me with a terrible trepidation that I could not even talk about with my parents. Even the sight of a flowing river frightened me if I imagined I must go and bathe in it. Eventually, with great resistance and after much emotional drama on my part, I learned to swim. With time, I developed an appreciation of the sea and learned to enjoy the benefits of swimming and playing in water. However, fear of the water has always stayed with me. I do not swim at night and I am rarely comfortable in deep water where I cannot see the bottom. Determined not to be controlled by my fear, I have spent a large amount of time in the water, even learning to scuba dive in order to master this irrational terror.

Once I began to investigate my past lives, I discovered several different occasions when I have died by drowning. I have drowned in rivers, ponds, oceans, and small streams. The water has captured and kept me on many occasions. Understanding my capacity as a soul to lose my life in water, I can better understand the enormous respect I have for the power of water to take life. Knowing my relationship with water, I can better understand the young girl I was, hesitating at the shoreline, observing my family playing so freely in the water as I worried about the waves claiming them. Reexperiencing the various deaths by drowning that I have experienced as a soul, has allowed me to develop a quality of trust and certainty about my desire to live in this life.

At the same time, I have recontacted the feeling of letting go into death, the surrender of physical life into immortality. The experience of death, rebirth, and death has shown me an aspect of myself that is beyond physical death. This experience helps me in daily life to let go of the past and to let old experiences and ideas I have about myself and others die.

Understanding that the relationship I have with water is unique to me and that I have a certain tendency to meet death in this way, I can better accept the timidity I feel about abandoning myself to the ocean. Using my fear of water as a catalyst for transformation, I have been able to recall my experiences of life after death—of the passage spent between lives, when I returned to light to integrate the experiences of life and prepare for my next incarnation.

• • •

Our past lives form part of the mysterious mosaic of who we are now in this current life. Access to past-life memories helps us to reassemble our sense of ourselves as diverse and multifaceted beings. Knowing where we come from and the path we have already traveled helps us to understand our true origins in light. The capacity to explore deaths we have already lived and in fact "survived," convinces us of our essentially immortal nature. The large perspective of ourselves that we gain from an exploration of past lives assists us in developing wisdom and tolerance, toward ourselves and toward others.

Finding the way to relive death, birth, and rebirth consciously opens our awareness to other planes of consciousness. The cycles of death and rebirth that we encounter in the deepness of our soul, lead us to a growing awareness of the existence of light as a healing, welcoming intelligence that accompanies us through both life and so-called death. We begin to perceive the operation of a guidance that follows our evolutionary path and to which we can refer for help, comfort and insight. The study of past lives and reincarnation leads us to the discovery of our spiritual guides, beings who assist us in our passages from life to death and back to life again, and who accompany us throughout all the adventures of our lives.

CHAPTER TWENTY-ONE

Spirit Guides

Spirit guides are beings, nonincarnated, who have a calling to assist in the evolutionary unfolding of the human race. They are guardians, angelic beings, messengers of truth, and very wise souls. Having been embodied themselves at some point in their evolutionary journey, they understand the human dilemma and the complex issues involved in living and creating on the material plane.

Their purpose, to guide humanity to light, is accomplished through working with individuals who are open and available to their presence. They never impose their presence or will upon another being—they come only by invitation, because of a sincere desire in the heart of the other to receive assistance and insight along the pathway to wholeness and remembering.

Spirit guides are teachers. They show us the way and they help us to remember what we need to know to find our way. They accompany us on our journey through life, but they cannot live our lives for us and they cannot interfere with our free will. When we make mistakes, our spirit guides may grieve with us but they will not stop us from going the way we have chosen. Guides understand our human need to learn through the experience of life, to acquire wisdom that can only grow through direct experience.

Spirit guides recognize humans as the rightful masters of the material plane. From their perspective, we are incarnated in the material world so that we can learn, in intricate detail, the laws of manifesting and manipulating physical matter. As living spirits, embodied, the Earth is our kingdom and we hold the greatest power. Guides follow our evolution with great and sincere interest and, when they perceive that we are available to enter into relationship with them, they will make their presence in our lives known to us.

In sessions of meditation when we are centered in our intuitive state of awareness, we begin to perceive the presence of our spirit guides with our inner senses. We feel ourselves enveloped in an atmosphere of warmth and healing and perceive a soft sense of presence. We may receive messages, guidance. Our guides may appear to us within our inner Temple, bringing us their teachings and the sacred gift of their presence in our inner world.

Our intuitive capacity allows us to perceive the presence of our guides and understand the significance of the teachings they have to offer us. Intuition serves as a bridge between the world of matter and the world of light where we are reunited with our guides.

CHANNELING

As we consecrate more and more of our time to the development of our intuitive capacity, we develop our ability to enter into communion with our spirit guides as well. The capacity to receive teachings from spirit guides is directly related to the intuitive function of knowingness or direct perception. When we receive messages in this manner, the process is known as channeling or transmission.

The capacity to channel is as innate to every human being as the capacity of intuition, but it is a skill that must be developed slowly and patiently over time and that must be practiced with a lot of discrimination. When we commit ourselves to the development of this capacity, we open ourselves up to other planes of existence and consciousness. It is essential to engage, at the same time, in a work of personal purification and transformation. We must develop strong qualities of wisdom, presence, and clarity, so that the transmissions we receive are of a high and pure quality. When we function in channeling mode, the transmissions we receive correspond to our inner energetic vibrations and to our personal and spiritual levels of evolution. Even though our guides are our teachers, and are thus more advanced than we are on the evolutionary wheel of illumination, the fact that they are our guides indicates that we resonate at a similar frequency. As we raise our energetic frequency to match theirs, communion with them becomes more frequent and communication becomes more fluid.

Communication with spirit guides allows us to receive spiritual teachings of a very high vibrational frequency, which can accelerate our personal evolution. Teachings transmitted to us by our guides assist us in very precise matters related to our incarnation and the problems we face along our evolutionary path. Spirit guides have the wonderful advantages of distance and detachment from worldly problems and their perspective can help us to understand and integrate the spiritual lessons we are learning in any given moment.

TRANSMISSIONS FROM MY SPIRIT GUIDES

Over the years I have been studying and working with the development of the intuition, I have also consecrated my time to the development of a relationship with spirit guides. The relationship has developed to the point where I am in regular contact with the light beings who accompany me through my life. They assist me on both a personal and professional level, offering me insight into my own evolution as well as guidance that assists in the evolution of students and clients. In the following pages are examples of some of these transmissions, demonstrating the presence, healing power, and deep wisdom of the light beings who watch over us all and accompany us on our evolutionary path.

Raphael

What is intuition?

❝Intuition is a way to connect your heart and your vision. With intuition you learn to speak truly, perceiving patterns of energy. You understand that you are part of a great totality and you see how the mind is limited.

In reading others, you discover your ability to go to the essential, to be detached, to understand what is connected to the essential movement of the person and what is not. Intuitive readings are a way to help people connect to their deepness, to their true desire.

Through intuitive development, you learn the importance of being real and authentic with yourself. Every time you speak the truth to another person, you create truth in yourself. Intuition teaches you to be thorough, to be clear, and to go beyond the mind. In finding your intuitive self, you reunite with the wisdom and the timelessness of your soul. With your inner senses, you touch the mysteries and paradoxes of being. You go beyond time and space into an inner state of emptiness where all truth is available to you. In this state you find the truth of yourself, and so, you find your place.❞

Istar

An invitation to enter into communion with the guides

❝Be not afraid of us, for we hold you close to our hearts and in all ways we wish light for you. We have been with you since eternity, waiting for your hearts and eyes to open to us, to recognize our presence in your lives. It is a great joy to us that now, many of you are becoming attuned to the world that is and is not—that you are dropping the rigidity of your thought-walls and letting us in.

Hear us—we have been entrusted with the great secrets, the truths you need to remember. In the softness of internal quiet, we can join you and tell you many things to assist you on your way.

See us—we are of the light, pure and clear, for we live in the heart of God and from Him, we come to you, clothed in His light, fresh with His love. We take the form known to you as human so that you can perceive us more clearly. For truly, it is our wish to assist you in love.

Know us—call us by the names we tell you. We can be with you in an instant of your time. Let us help you. It is our calling to guide you. There are many of us, yet we are in truth but one. We are a mirroring of you, we are the light of you, untouched by matter. We are truly free, but for our love of you, and this love binds us to your purpose.

Feel us—we touch you, we bring you gifts of healing light and weave them all around you, enfolding you in His light and love. We know your pain and your joy and we await you patiently—we know you are coming home. The journey is long and you become weary, but listen . . . listen with your hearts . . . the very sky opens to welcome you. His heart draws you, warming you. You are almost home.

In these days, in these very special days, we have much to teach you, much to show you. The light now is bright and we are welcome in many hearts.

Remember us—we are your friends, and we are beloveds of the true light. Be at peace, beloveds, for beloveds you are. You have not been forgotten. Your light shines and grows, and love is here in the healing you give. Trust."

Ariel and Raphael

A teaching about fear, purification, and transformation

❝When we come to you, we speak to your consciousness, to your soul. It is through the consciousness of your soul that we are in contact with you.

Your soul, which was hidden in the deepness of your heart, expands and takes its place throughout your body. Every time you accept light, you nourish your soul and your soul grows and becomes more radiant, more luminous, more lucid, and more powerful. As you allow your soul-consciousness to awaken and expand your awareness, you have many revelations about who you are, where you come from, and about your capacities.

Because you have answered our call, you are an instrument of light. You are a soul who has accepted the task of awakening others to the truth of who they are.

To become free is a process of liberating yourself from fear. Fear is the greatest limitation. The fear of letting go is a fear written deeply into the cells of your physical body. The body believes that fear helps it to survive. For the body, fear is essential to survival. Fear and protection are almost the same thing to the body. Fear is a quality of energy, a belief passed down through the generations of the family. The family story of fear is contained in the kidneys. The fears of the mother and the fears of the father act together to create the fears of the infant. Think about the fact that the water of the uterus is a water coming from the mother. Water is connected to the kidneys and kidneys are associated with ancestral stories and the survival of the family. The fetus is protected by the water, but the water, in itself, is connected to the quality of fear.

It is difficult to separate life from fear. Fear creates limits and life seems full of limits. This dilemma is one of the greatest challenges on the path of revelation of the truth of who you really are. To go beyond fear and the limitations imposed by fear, you must have a warrior's spirit. You must dare to face your fear, to overcome your fear, and to go beyond it. But you must understand that the fear you face is not simply your personal fear. It is the fears of the family, the fears of your ancestors, the fears held within you from old incarnations you have lived. The only place in you where you are beyond fear is in the consciousness of your soul and spirit. In this place, fear is nonexistent, because there are no limits, because you are living in the consciousness of your immortality.

Fear is matter in the absence of light-consciousness. Fear is you living in the illusion of mortality. Fear is you thinking you are your physical body and your personality. Fear is the result of the great illusion of separation and ego.

You are in the process of liberating yourself from fear and from this illusion. You are eliminating the fear of your ancestral heritage. You are freeing yourself from the past, from your karmic story. This process is experienced as an elimination. Liberation from fear triggers many physical symptoms and reactions. You must understand that, in a sense, your body has a life of its own. The instinct to survive is very strong. The paradox is that this instinct to survive is what ultimately causes death of the physical body.

When each and every cell of your physical body is incarnated with the living light of your soul-consciousness, you become immortal, you become free. To become free in this fashion, all fear must be purified, transformed, and liberated with the consciousness of your light self.

You must accept the fear which is there, but which is not really you. You must become the master of your body, accepting the presence of fear without becoming dominated by it. Your body has fear and fear creates pain and illness. So, like a wise and loving parent, you take the fearful child into your heart, accepting and listening to the story of the fear. But you do not think that you are the fear. You accept that the fear is there and, with the energy of loving wisdom, you dissolve the fear. You free the child from its fear by revealing the fear as an illusion. You bring light to the place of fear. The light absorbs the shadow and so the fear is dissolved, creating more place for light. In a place of light, the soul is free and can live in truth and freedom.

As the light inhabits you more and more fully, your healing abilities become more powerful and your inner vision becomes more clear. Do not underestimate the purifying power of light. Do not become discouraged by the feeling of not knowing where you are going. In your soul, you know where you are going. You are going home. You are leaving forever the structures and frameworks of the illusions through which you have functioned since eternity. You are liberating yourself from limitations. You are mastering physical matter and you are transforming this matter, returning matter to light. This alchemical process is happening first and foremost in the physical matter of your body. Every time you touch matter with the intention of transforming it to light, a movement of elimination, purification, and transformation is triggered.

You can renounce your past and the path of illusion, but do not renounce your experience. Your experience is priceless. Your experience is your truth and your truth is who you are. Believe us when we say to you, with great love and compassion, that you will need all your experience to help you, to guide you and to guide others, in these coming years of transition, in these years of purification. We are sorry that this period of transition is difficult to live through. You are not yet capable of living in the eternal blessing of light-consciousness. God is here in light and in light is His love. His great love is eternal and you too are the essence of eternal love. Open yourself to love, to light and to the God-essence. We thank you."

Red Eagle

*Speaking about his human life, his human death, and
preparation for death from this world*

"I am an old man. I am old and dry. My bones are dry and I am
waiting for the wind to take me. My heart is heavy. My heart is
sad. I sit on my rock and I wait for the wind to take me. Facing me,
I see the land. The land is rich and full of life. The sky is vast. The
Sun is here. I breathe with the Earth. I am waiting. I am waiting for
the Earth to let me go. I am waiting for the Earth to release me.
Soon, the Earth will expire and I will leave. The Sun will breathe me
and the wind will take me and from this Earth. I will disappear. I
love this Earth but I will not be sorry to leave. My people have gone,
I am old, and I wait for the wind to come for me.

It was not easy to live and see all that I have seen. It was not an
easy time to walk upon this Earth. I have survived even my death. I
lived my death and I am still alive.

Do not be afraid to die. You cannot escape the experience. You
cannot escape, so you may as well surrender. I will help you to be
courageous in front of your death. It will help you to be courageous
if you can remember that death is like breathing. In this moment,
you breathe with the Earth and you are in the arms of your Mother
Earth. Your mother breathes and you live. The Great Spirit released
you from his heart so that you could go and live with your mother,
the Earth. He gave you to the mother so that she could love you. So
that she could know you. So that she could carry you in her heart.

The Great Father is generous. He gives his children to the
mother. He is generous. But there is a moment when he wishes for
his children to come back to him. He lends you to the Earth, but the
Great Father needs you too. When you are gone, he misses you. He
lets you go. He knows one day you will come back. He waits for you.
He knows when you come back you will tell him many stories. You

will speak of your experiences. He is old now. The Great Father is very old. Your legs are stronger than his. You can do long journeys and so you have many stories to tell.

One day he cannot let you stay longer. He takes a great breath and he draws you back to him. He breathes as the wind and he carries you back to him. He breathes you in. You expire with your breath and you leave this Earth. The Mother Earth lets you go. She cannot do anything else. They have an agreement, the Great Father and the mother, and each must honor the agreement.

You can be happy to find yourself back in the heart of the Great Father. He is like your Sun. He is warm and generous. He is a loving father, a kind father. You can be sad to leave the Earth, your mother, because she is warm and soft, but when you find yourself back with the father you will forget your sorrow. You will be joyful.

Do not be afraid of what you call death. I am old and my bones are dry, and I am still alive. What I learned in the journey of my death was to accept my sorrow. You have never met a man as sorry as I. You cannot know the depth of my sorrow.

Do not let your sorrow make you bitter. This is my advice to you. Do not let your sorrow stop you from seeing the joy. There is much joy. There is as much joy as there is sadness.

I was a man with a position. I was a man with a place. I was a man with many children; many wives and many children. All of my people were lost to me. They were all taken from me. You cannot ask a man to bear more sorrow than that. It is true, I was bitter. How can the Great Father be so cruel? How can he be so hard?

We were a great people, it is true. It is not easy to understand why a people must perish, that something so fine could be destroyed because of ignorance.

I was, in my time, a wise man. I was a man who knew nature, who spoke with spirits. I was what you would call a medicine man. In front of the changes of that time, I was important. You were also alive in that time, in that hard time of losing. Do not try to understand that time. We lost many of our children. It was so sad. These children died to us, but they did not die. Do not hold this bitterness in your hearts. Do not become dry like me. Our children died, but it was to go back to the father. Now I understand that, but in my bitterness, I could not accept it. I am an old and dry man, almost as dry as the wind now. You must let your sorrow flow. The sorrow in your heart is like your lifeblood. You must release it and let it flow. You must not become dry. You must stay fluid.

You cannot change the ways of the gods. You cannot understand the ways of the gods. They have their movement. They have their stories and we are part of their stories. Their story is much bigger than we are. Now, where I am, I understand this better. There is as much joy as there is sadness. That is the truth. The children die, but the children also live. They laugh. They play.

One day you will die to this Earth. That is inevitable. It cannot be another way. When it is your time to die, try not to be bitter. If you are bitter, it will be difficult to open your heart. It will be difficult to open your heart to say good-bye to the mother and it will be difficult to open your heart to say hello to the father. When your heart is open, you can breathe easily, you can go from life, you can go to death, and you can go to life again, simply. Do not forget that, my children.

When you see the moment of your death arriving, you must remember to open yourself. You will live your life, and then, you will live your death like a birth, like a new life. I am an old man. I have walked a long way on your Earth. Like all old men, I have many memories. I thank you for listening to an old man.

I bless you with the love of the father. I bless you with the love of the mother. May the mother show you your path and the father bring you his Sun. May you always go in peace. And may the wind carry you gently home."

Kwan Yin

A teaching about the healer within

"Greetings to you, my beloved sisters and brothers. My purpose in speaking to you is to tell you about healing. I am a teacher of healing. I am a being who has consecrated her existence to the work of healing. I have been working for many, many centuries of your time.

Perhaps, in the deepness of your soul, you can remember me, not as a person but as a presence. I am a sister of God. I am a sister of love and a sister of mercy. The vibration of my being is in relation to the colors of rose and green. My name is Kwan Yin. In your world, I am venerated as a goddess. I am that, but more than that, I am a spirit. I am a being. I am a teacher of love.

It is my duty to teach healing and to raise the awareness of beings such as you, so that you may take your place in the world as healers. We are many working together to realize our goal of planetary healing.

A healer is what you already are. You are not learning to be a healer. You are remembering yourself as the healer that you are. Healing is not a technique, even though there are many techniques that you can learn which will help you in your work. You are a healer because of who you are in your deepness. You must absolutely become aware of and accept this fact.

It is your presence that heals. It is your energy that heals. Your existence provokes healing in others. Because of who you are, it is like that. There is a movement in you, a very special movement. You have a special connection with light, with God. This connection is written in your soul. It is something decided before you were born into this life. Before you took this body, you consecrated your life to healing.

You have devoted yourself to the path of healing because you understand that there is no other way. You understand that to help others is truly an honorable path. You understand that there is a great work to do. You understand that everyone must cooperate together. You understand that the suffering of the other is your suffering. You understand that the joy of the other is your joy. You understand all these things, very important things. Because of your understanding you have consecrated your life to healing.

Now you must assume responsibility for the vow you have taken. You have a connection in you, with us, with the world of energy, the world of spirits, of guides, of light. We act through you. Because of your contact with us, there is a large movement within you. This movement touches others, provokes others into their own movement.

If you do not use your gift of healing, you will find yourself overcome by your problems. You cannot stop the movement. You can only go with the movement. Many of the problems you think you have are the result of yourself stopping this movement. Your attention is too much on yourself. You are too preoccupied with your small problems. You think you should solve your problems before you can help others. But I tell you, that it is not the way. You must abandon yourself to the movement, abandon yourself to light, abandon yourself to us. Give yourself to the service of helping others. In this way, you will find your movement. Others will find their movement, and you will liberate yourself from your obsessions.

Your problems are not important. They are illusions. You are not your problems. You create your problems because of your mental obsessions. Your thoughts create. Everything you create with your thoughts is an illusion. Illusion that seems very real. Problems that seem very serious. With all of these problems, which seem so serious, you think you cannot begin to help others, because first you must help yourself. You are in a trap.

What you must understand is that only when you begin to help others can we truly begin to help you. When you let go of all your obsessions of your small world, you are opening yourself to the vastness of the big world.

A healer is not something you learn to be. It is something you already are. You are that. Look at your life and you will see that it is evident. You are a healer. You have something in you that calls other people to come to you. They ask for your help. They speak to you. They open their hearts to you. They open their lives to you. Look at yourself. Look at your life. You have always been doing that. If people come to you, opening their hearts to you, it is because, instinctively, they trust you. Be aware of yourself, of who you are.

We do not ask you to heal alone. It is the contrary. We ask you to open yourself to us. We ask you to work in collaboration with us. You are our hands. You are our eyes. You have nothing to fear from our presence. We share the same goal. Simply, we are here in light and you are there in matter.

We are very grateful to you that you have chosen to be incarnated in this period of time. You are many. You must nourish each other. There is much work to do. There is a great work to accomplish. There are many hearts to touch, many souls to care for, many beings to wake up. This is your task. It was your obsession from the beginning.

You can only be who you are. We do not ask you more than that. We ask only that you be who you are and that you achieve your goals, that you participate. Do not think that you are alone. Truly, we are never far from you. We are with you. We heal you. We heal the others. We love you so much. We thank you.

We wish you would let yourself really see. Try not to be discouraged by the difficulties. The more you can abandon yourself to light, the more the light can carry you to your goal. The more you can abandon yourself to light, the more the other can be healed simply by being in your presence.

You are not responsible for the enlightenment of others. As a healer, your responsibility lies in helping others to find their own movement, helping others to wake up to the truth of who they are. You help them to find the resources within themselves which they need to heal themselves. You are not responsible for their enlightenment.

My children, do not be discouraged by what you think is happening in this world of yours. It is not as bad as all that. The world is healing. All your people are healing. Slowly, the beings are awakening. Do not be discouraged. We are not discouraged. We are very hopeful.

You are our children. But more than our children, you are our brothers and sisters and we are waiting for you. One day you will come back to us. After your task is done, you will come back to us to rest in light. But do not be in a hurry to come back to us. There is no need. We can be with you where you are. The work that you accomplish has a purpose. Every time you touch the heart of another, there is more joy in this world. Every time you act from your truth, you are bringing more love into this world. Every moment is sacred, every gesture is important, every action has a consequence. Every moment you are in your own awareness, you bring this world to awareness. You have a place in that, my children. You have a role to play and we thank you. We thank you for your willingness, for your courage, for your caring.

I thank you for listening to me. I thank you for your presence. It is my need to speak. In speaking, I know I can touch you in your heart. In speaking, I know you will begin to remember who I am. In remembering me, you remember yourself. You remember your origins. In remembering who you are, you can remember why you are here.

Blessings to you."

Ariel

A teaching about light, the light that we are, the Sun, and the quality of intention

66 There are not many people who are called to do this work that we give you. We have waited patiently for a long time until we have found the right atmosphere.

To understand light, the real nature of light, you must be willing to let go all of your ideas about light. You are light.

In fact, it is very simple: because you are light, you cannot see yourself clearly. What you perceive as yourself is simply the structure that contains the light. You are the light that exists between the structure of matter, but you cannot touch this light. It is a light so fine, so light, that you cannot grasp it. Light is your original nature. Light is your essence. It is natural that you take light for granted. Your true father, the Sun, has always blessed you with his light. He is light . . . he is a light that is dying. Still, see how he is beautiful, how he is nourishing you with his warmth, and how, with his grace, life flourishes.

Your light is more than the light of the Sun. We know that you cannot understand this. Your light is a living light, a conscious light, a light with a purpose, with intention. It is this intention that makes you great. With this intention, your light magnifies light.

You have the power, not only to send light, but to create light. Do not be discouraged by your smallness. Your fragility is an essential aspect of your true beauty. The light that you are is precious, more precious than anything on Earth.

You come from a source that is beyond description. You carry within you the memory of the source and the pathway home. But do not be in a hurry to come back to us, for truly, you have a place on Earth. You have a work to do and we are with you. We never leave you. Even when you are lost, we are with you.

We speak always to the light in you, the light of your infinite intelligence. You have forgotten much about that which you truly are, but in your deepness, you remember all that is essential to bring you home.

Be courageous. Stay in trust. The light that is in your heart-of-hearts is your true guide. Believe in yourself. Stay available. We are with you."

CHAPTER TWENTY-TWO

Going the Way of the White Clouds

We are going the way of the white clouds,
we are going the way of the white clouds,
Home to You, Home to You.

—Sufi song

The transmissions from the spirit guides are full of hope, blessings, and patient encouragement. The guides are wise and their teachings are offered in an atmosphere of love, encouragement, and understanding. After a session of channeling, I am deeply touched in my heart, moved by the teachings I have received and also by the quality of relationship I feel with the guides. Their presence helps me to remember who I am, where I come from, and to where, eventually, I will return.

The guides exist on another vibrational plane—a plane of light, radiance, and soft welcoming warmth. Thanks to intuitive perception, the gap between the everyday physical world and their world of light is bridged and, for the time that we are in communication, our two worlds can meet. Contact with my world teaches the guides about the pleasures and dilemmas of being human; contact with theirs reveals to me again and again that light is the essence of creation, an ever present force completely permeating our world and the precious experience we call life.

Thanks to my meetings with the guides, I receive a living teaching about light, personal transformation, and human evolution that I can apply in my daily life, as well as in my professional vocation.

The teachings of the guides are perfectly adapted to spiritual seekers committed to life in the material world. They help us to develop discipline, detachment and skills of self-realization, while, at the same time we learn the art of letting go into silence, heart, and communion. One of the ultimate purposes of the guides is to assist people on a path of spiritual evolution to develop their capacity to enter into intuitive contact with their own guides. In this period of transition toward the new millennium, we need guidance. We need wisdom and we need perspective. The presence of spirit guides does not allow us to escape from the world or to go beyond being human, but rather helps us to be, and to become, the beings that we potentially are in our deepest selves.

The path I have taken is a path of learning. First as student, then as teacher, and, as teacher, always student. Of all the tools I have acquired throughout my years of learning, it is my intuition that has been the most valuable.

The intuition is the beginning and the end, it is the essence, the answer. The intuition opens the door to the truth, to the vast mysteries of existence, and to the equally vast mysteries of the human being.

We are all intuitive. Of this I am certain. However, intuition is not always an easy gift to carry. To perceive the truth in the midst of lies causes deep sadness. To carry awareness of the long path traveled by the soul can be tiring, at times an oppressive weight to bear. To perceive and feel the sadness, fear, and suffering of others is heartrending, almost too much to bear. To be so sensitive—to feel, to see, to know—at times, it is hard to be all that and still be gay, vibrant, laughing.

But intuitive we are and we cannot be another way. It is our birthright, our inheritance. It is part of our depth, our fragility, and our ultimate strength and beauty. To refuse our intuition is to refuse ourselves. To refuse ourselves, we are condemned to a lost and lonely life, cut off from our hearts, cut off from feeling, and cut off from the source from which we have come.

Reconciliation with our intuition brings us home to ourselves and, in coming home to ourselves, we come home to the divinity within. We rediscover our deepness, our vast potential, and the endless mystery of ourselves.

In aligning ourselves with our intuition, we give birth to the marriage between the masculine and feminine living within us. We create a movement of inner alchemy and, once this movement is activated, we will never again be the same. Intuition brings us to independence and inner reliance. We are able to seek our own counsel, to find the answers to our questions within ourselves in the calm, silent temple of the inner soul. The ultimate gift of the intuition is the gift of homecoming. Coming home to ourselves, we come to our appropriate place, to our true purpose.

We have, each and every one of us, a reason for living—we have a purpose. It is this purpose that we must discover and then realize in order to accomplish the evolution of our soul. One day, we will die to this world and we will return to the light from which we came. But the essential being that we are, the consciousness of our spirit and soul, is eternal and will remember the path we have traveled long after our bodies have gone to dust. Our origins are in light and our intuition is the incarnation of our light nature in all its power, wisdom, and truth. By giving a place to our intuition we heal ourselves of ancient wounds and old, old sorrows. We give a place to joy, laughter, and knowingness. We give a place to our heart and we allow our wisdom to live within us. Guided in love and protected by wisdom, we are sure to find our path all the way home.

The School of Intuition Development

It is more difficult to advance alone on a path of personal transformation than it is to share the journey with other like-minded souls who are adventuring along in the same direction. It is partly for this reason that we have witnessed the huge growth of classes, courses, groups, and trainings in personal development over the past two decades throughout the Western world. People come together to learn, and they discover that joining together and sharing a common goal is enriching and heartwarming. The collective energy generated by a group creates an atmosphere that is particularly fertile for personal development.

Within the group dynamic, we find a world rich in the potential of interpersonal relationships, a world where we are far away from daily social obligations and habits, a place where we can drop masks and images. We find ourselves in a very privileged atmosphere, an atmosphere in which we are encouraged to devote ourselves to the discovery, exploration, and realization of our inner potential. Away from home and the routines of daily life, group work offers a retreat during which we can heal ourselves and reconnect with the inner resources that help us to construct and effectively manage our daily lives.

Giving ourselves some precious time in a privileged atmosphere, we are more able to concentrate on the inner process of personal transformation that occurs during the unfolding of the group. We create new habits and make inner resolutions that we will practice and integrate into our lives when we return home.

The techniques and practical exercises proposed throughout these pages have all been drawn from the program of training of The Intuition School. Originally taught through a series of evening classes, the training has evolved into a program of forty-two days, taught on weekends and in modules of several days. The time spent "in school" is completely devoted to the development of the intuition. The program is comprehensive, drawn from a wide range of body/mind transformational techniques, to ensure a result that is tangible and that can be effectively utilized in daily life.

The program is organized into three levels or modules. Students advance level by level, integrating each phase of the work before moving on to the next more advanced stage of development. In the first level of the training, we concentrate on inner preparation and personal transformation. During the second level, we learn specific techniques associated with intuitive perception and psychic healing. The final phase is devoted to spiritual healing, both in relation to self and the healing path in a more professional context.

Essentially experiential in nature, the program is taught through a continuous process of explanation, demonstration, practice, and subsequent sharing and feedback. The progress of each student in the group is followed individually, with personal supervision when appropriate, to assist in the transformation of obstacles blocking the expression of the intuition.

THE PROGRAM

Level I: Self-awareness and Inner Clarity

(10 DAYS)

These seminars teach the fundamental skills indispensable to the development of the intuition. Meditation and self-healing techniques are incorporated into a body/mind awareness training which leads to deep personal transformation and inner reconciliation.

- The four pathways of the intuition
- Centering and inner silence
- Trust
- Thought is creative
- Intuitive decision making
- Inner vision
- The energetic body
- The chakras
- Symbolic images and their transformation
- Self-healing
- Transformation of belief systems
- Acceptation and forgiveness
- Inner alchemy
- Manifesting techniques

Level II: Intuition and Relating to Others

(14 DAYS)

In the second level, you learn the practical techniques of intuitive reading and psychic healing. Practicing with other participants, the intuition is stimulated and empowered. You develop trust and confidence, and rediscover your sense of purpose in life. Exploring the power and truth of the intuition as a catalyst for transformation, you experience your intuitive capacity as a sacred aspect of the soul, to be respected and honored.

- The structure of emotion
- The art of subtle perception
- Intuitive readings of the physical and energetic bodies
- Chakra readings
- Relationship readings
- The principles of psychic healing
- Transmitting qualities
- Presence and compassion
- Past lives
- Soul reading
- Life purpose
- Spirit guides

Level III: Offering Your Gift to the World

(18 DAYS)

The synthesis of the training allows each individual to access and understand their personal healing gift and develop the means to express it in the world. Intensive practice refines and further develops the intuitive skill, while personal supervision aids participants to realize their unique ways to utilize the intuition in daily life. Reconciliation with the wisdom of the heart and spiritual healing of the soul clarifies life-purpose, bringing certainty, freedom, and true autonomy.

- Rightful place
- Inner balance
- Original innocence
- Power and justice
- Alignment to the vertical
- Letting go
- Spiritual healing
- Faithfulness to the intuitive being
- Divine love
- Warrior's spirit, healer's heart
- Intervention strategies in relation to needs
- Practice and perfection of intuitive techniques
- Frameworks for professional practice
- Ethics and integrity

For further information on The Intuition Training, please contact:

Judee Gee
Consciousness Academy
Les Martets
84490 St. Saturnin Les Apt
France

Tel/Fax: +33 (0)4 90 75 58 78

email: judee.gee@wanadoo.fr

Suggested Reading List

Balsekar, Ramesh, S. *Consciousness Speaks: Conversations with Ramesh S. Balsekar.* Redondo Beach, CA: Advaita Press, 1992.

Brennan, Barbara Ann. *Hands of Light: A Guide to Healing Through the Human Energy Field.* New York: Bantam Books, 1988.

Carey, Ken. *Starseed Transmissions.* San Francisco: HarperSanFrancisco, 1992.

———. *Return of the Bird Tribes.* San Francisco: HarperSanFrancisco, 1992.

Chia, Mantak. *Awaken Healing Energy Through the Tao.* Santa Fe: Aurora Press, 1981.

Chopra, Deepak. *Ageless Body, Timeless Mind: A Practical Alternative to Growing Old.* London: Rider Books, 1993; and New York: Crown, 1995.

Douglas, Nik, and Penny Slinger. *Sexual Secrets: The Alchemy of Ecstasy.* Rochester, VT: Destiny Books, 1979.

Estés, Clarissa Pinkola. *The Faithful Gardener.* San Francisco: HarperSanFrancisco, 1995.

Gibran, Kahlil. *The Prophet.* New York: Knopf, 1987.

Grof, Christina, and Stanislav Grof, M.D. *The Stormy Search for Self: A Guide to Personal Growth Through Transformational Crisis.* Los Angeles: Jeremy Tarcher, 1992.

Hay, Louise. *The Power Is Within You.* Carson, CA: Hay House, 1991.

————. *Heal Your Body*. Carson, CA: Hay House, 1988.

Hoff, Benjamin. *The Tao of Pooh*. New York: E. P. Dutton, 1987.

Houston, Jean. *The Possible Human*. Los Angeles: Jeremy Tarcher, 1982.

Joy, Brugh W., M.D. *Joy's Way: A Map for the Transformational Journey*. Los Angeles: Jeremy Tarcher, 1979.

Klimo, Jon. *Channeling: Investigations on Receiving Information from Paranormal Sources*. Berkeley, CA: North Atlantic Books, 1997.

Kornfield, Jack. *A Path With Heart*. New York: Bantam, 1993.

Leboyer, Frédérick. *Birth Without Violence*. London: Wildwood House, 1979; Rochester, VT: Inner Traditions, 1995.

Levine, Stephen and Ondrea. *Embracing the Beloved: Relationship as a Path of Awakening*. New York: Doubleday, 1996; and Bath, England: Gateway, 1996.

Manné, Joy. *Soul Therapy*. Berkeley, CA: North Atlantic Books, 1997.

Minett, Gunnel. *Breath and Spirit: Rebirthing as a Healing Technique*. London: Aquarian Press, 1994.

Mission Control Staff and Zoev IHO Staff. *E. T. 101: The Cosmic Instruction Manual for Planetary Evolution*. New York: HarperCollins, 1995; and London: Thorsons, 1995.

Moore, Thomas. *Care of the Soul*. London: Piatkus, 1992; and New York: HarperPerennial Library, 1994.

Morgan, Marla. *Mutant Message Down Under*. London: Thorsons, 1994; and New York: HarperCollins, 1994.

Morningstar, Jim, Ph.D. *Breathing in Light and Love: Your Call to Breath and Body Mastery*. Milwaukee, WI: Transformations Incorporated, 1994.

Osho. *The Psychology of the Esoteric*. Cologne, Germany: The Rebel Publishing House, 1997.

————. *Tantra—The Supreme Understanding*. Pune, India: The Rebel Publishing House, 1998.

Ray, Sondra and Bob Mandel. *Birth and Relationships: How Your*

Birth Affects Your Relationships. Berkeley, CA: Celestial Arts, 1987.

Rinpoche, Sogyal. *The Tibetan Book of Living and Dying*. San Francisco: HarperSanFrancisco, 1994.

Rogers, Carl R. *On Becoming a Person*. Boston: Houghton Mifflin, 1972.

Schumacher, E. F. *A Guide for the Perplexed*. New York: Harper-Collins, 1978.

Shah, Idries. *The Way of the Sufi*. Middlesex, England: Penguin Arkana, 1968.

Starhawk. *Spiral Dance: A Rebirth of the Ancient Religion of the Great Goddess*. San Francisco: HarperSanFrancisco, 1979.

Trungpa, Chogyam. *Cutting Through Spiritual Materialism*. Boston: Shambhala, 1973.

Lao Tzu. *Tao Te Ching*. New York: Bantam Books, 1990.

Walker, Pete. *The Tao of Fully Feeling: Harvesting Forgiveness Out of Blame*. Lafayette, CA: Azure Coyote Publishing, 1995.

Watts, Alan. *The Way of Zen*. New York: Vintage Books, 1989.

Yogananda, Paramahansa. *Autobiography of a Yogi*. Los Angeles: Self Realization Fellowship, 1979.

Index

Judee Gee is the creator and director of The Intuition School (L'Ecole de l'Intuition) in France where she has been based for the last ten years. Her intuition development program is particularly oriented toward professional therapists and healers seeking further training in intuitive perception as well as personal re-sourcing and transformation. She lectures and teaches throughout France on themes related to spiritual healing and self-realization. Born and raised in Australia, she was trained in intuitive perception, psychic healing, and transformational breathwork in the San Francisco Bay area, where she lived and taught for several years during the 1980s. For close to twenty years she has been intensively involved in research concerning breath, consciousness, and spiritual purification, and is currently Chairwoman of the International Breathwork Foundation, a global networking organization for people interested in Breathwork. Known for a teaching style that combines simplicity, wit, and wisdom, she also facilitates teacher training in the field of intuitive development.